Hands-On Healing

ALSO BY
GLENN R. MOSLEY

Living Life in the Key of "R"

The Association of Unity Churches International (coauthored)

New Thought, Ancient Wisdom

Wake Up…Live the Life You Love (coauthored)

The Power of Prayer Around the World (coauthored)

Unity: Wings Across Time (coedited)

Dying, Death, and Grieving (coauthored)

Secular and Religious Instructional Games Compared

Unity Methods of Self-Exploration

Learning to Live with People

Hands-On Healing
Simple Steps to Health and Wholeness

———(o)———

GLENN R. MOSLEY

SENTIENT PUBLICATIONS

Cover design by Kim Johansen
Book design by Timm Bryson

Library of Congress Cataloging-in-Publication Data

Mosley, Glenn.
Hands-on healing : simple steps to health and wholeness / by Glenn R. Mosley.–
1st Sentient Publications ed.
p. cm.
Includes bibliographical references.
ISBN 1-59181-048-5
1. Touch–Therapeutic use. 2. Imposition of hands–Therapeutic use. 3. Vital
force–Therapeutic use. I. Title.
RZ999.M68 2006
615.8'51–dc22
                                        2005037616
Printed in the United States of America

10 9 8 7 6 5 4 3 2 1

SENTIENT PUBLICATIONS, LLC
1113 Spruce Street
Boulder, CO 80302
www.sentientpublications.com

Contents

———(o)———

CONTENTS

CONTENTS

Foreword

Today, more than 40 percent of people in the United States use some form of alternative or complementary medical therapy to help in the treatment of physical diseases. Spiritual techniques like prayer are commonly included among these therapies. Healing touch is another practice that is increasingly being used in a variety of clinical settings.

Glenn R. Mosley is the president and CEO emeritus of the Association of Unity Churches International. In this book, he describes the technique of Healing Hover Touch and the amazing results that he has seen using this method. In 1962, four decades ago, Dr. Mosley began sharing this gift with others. Here he reveals for the first time how he discovered and refined this healing technique over many years of trial and practice. He is truly an authority on the topic, having during the past thirty-plus years lectured about and performed Healing Hover Touch around the United States and in many countries of the world. Dr. Mosley indicates that, using this technique, he has detected illnesses (like cancer) that even physicians were unable to identify after careful and comprehensive examination.

Briefly, the technique of Healing Hover Touch involves placing the hands about two to three inches above the subject's body and moving them around the body from head to toe, front to back, sensing areas of unhealthy energy accumulation; then the practitioner rebalances the body's energy to achieve a more healthy equilibrium. Before the practitioner performs this technique, however, he or she must spend time heart centering. To Dr. Mosley, this is the most important step. It involves developing one's prayer life in order to serve as a clear vessel of love and goodwill, and then visualizing the highest good for the client.

The second step involves assessment, wherein the healer passes his or her hands over the client's front and back, head to toe, identifying areas of hot or cold that need attention. Next, clearing and upgrading are used to balance out these areas of Qi (or *chi*) accumulation or deficit; this process produces healing in the pathology that underlies these areas of imbalance in the Qi. Finally, the healer uses the hands to achieve closure, sealing the body's chakras so that positive energy is not lost.

Dr. Mosley describes extraordinary cases of healings that have been brought about by Healing Hover Touch, and he also answers frequently asked questions about the technique. This book is easy to read and enlightening, and it will surely provide hope to those who are experiencing conditions that traditional medicine has been unable to help. Glenn Mosley is a sensitive and articulate spokesperson for a technique that may help free many from unnecessary pain and suffering.

—Harold G. Koenig, M.D., author
The Healing Power of Faith

Preface

The information provided between these covers is meant to augment both your awareness and understanding of natural remedies and is not intended to either diagnose or treat the health problems of any individual, nor to replace medical recommendations of physicians or other health professionals.

On the contrary, the information here is provided to help you work with the various health-care providers and physicians of your choice for the best possible outcome regarding your health. There could be risks in relation to some of the natural remedies considered in these pages, just as surely as there may be risks in relation to prescribed drugs or other modalities of medical treatment. For that reason, before you begin any kind of natural remedy, consult your own health-care practitioner. Also, do not discontinue any course of medical treatment or therapy you may now be undergoing without consulting your health-care professional.

Appropriate medical care is essential to good health; do not self-diagnose. If you think you have symptoms of an illness discussed in this book—or *any* illness—please consult a health-care professional. You may want to consider a holistic Doctor of

Osteopathy (D.O.), a holistic Advanced Registered Nurse Practitioner (ARNP), a Doctor of Naturopathy (N.D.), a Doctor of Homeopathy, (Hom.D.), a Doctor of Chiropractic (D.C.)—especially those who include acupuncture, Nambudripads Allergy Elimination Techniques (NAET), or reflexology as treatment alternatives, a holistic Doctor of Medicine (M.D.), or other natural-health-care provider. For household pets and other domesticated animals in your care, see Appendix A under American Holistic Veterinary Medical Association.

In addition to using the health-care services of an allopathic physician (M.D.), if you want to try one of the myriad alternative, complementary, or integrative (all three of which are often called simply *alternative*) approaches, discuss it with your health-care provider. In the following pages, I will explain the evolution of medical terms and why I primarily use the term *integrative*. Thereafter, I will use the term *integrative* or an elongated form of it.

If you are presently on prescribed medication, you must work with your physician before you discontinue any drug. To do otherwise could be life-threatening or, at the very least, could be an impediment to progress in your healing process.

No matter which, or how many, of the integrative medical and natural remedy approaches you choose (including vitamins, herbs, and minerals) to assist you in maintaining and regaining health, a diet that feeds your body and a wholesome lifestyle that feeds the mind and spirit are absolutely essential to wholeness.

The identities of the people described and the testimonies given in the following pages have been changed to preserve confidentiality (except in instances where specific permission has been granted by clients and workshop participants to the author to do otherwise). In some instances, multiple stories of single individuals have been combined into a graphic composite.

Neither the author nor the publisher is responsible for services or products referred to in this book, and both parties expressly disclaim any and all liability regarding fulfillment of services of any such products and for loss, damage, or expense whatsoever either to property or person arising out of or relating to them.

Acknowledgments

—— (o) ——

My thanks to those who helped with this manuscript, colleagues and friends all. Lisa Wittman and Cary Herold provided assistance with the Association of Unity Churches' survey named in the list of references. Also, thanks to Kim Shawd, Al Sears, and Marsha Penrose—model, photographer, and artist, respectively—for the illustrations in Chapter 4, "Instructions for Balancing Body Energy in Healing Hover Touch." My thanks for editing assistance and the typing of the first couple of drafts to Sandra duMonde. Minister and allopathic physician Dr. Carl Osier, and my executive assistant, Bets Kirby, both offered suggestions and assistance with editing portions of the manuscript. Thanks, also, in this area, to Episcopal priest, psychiatrist, and friend Dr. John O'Hearne, along with my gratitude to colleagues Dr. Larry Dossey and Dr. Harold Koenig for their friendship and their thoughts along the way. Thank you especially to Rev. Rebekah Dunlap for her suggestions, editing, and production wizardry.

I appreciate the feedback and help from tens of thousands who have participated in both my healing workshops (learning experiences) and surveys. I am grateful to those who have shared with me as I conducted classes and facilitated learning experiences in hospital in-services; nursing residences; retreats; churches; synagogues; civic and corporate groups; seminary courses; clubs; and regional, national, and international conventions and conferences, both of church denominations and medical disciplines. I wish to specifically include in this list the Spring 1998 National Conference of the American Academy of Family Physicians (and their invited international delegate-guests). Each of the above has been both student and teacher to me.

Finally, thanks to Martha, my wife—also a friend, a marriage and family therapist, and a colleague—for her support in my facilitating those innumerable learning weeks and weekends that have taught me so much.

Introduction

While it appears that the world is undergoing a spiritual revolution and that the church is not leading it, it may also be that a medical-wellness revolution is under way and that the traditional medical disciplines are not leading it, either.

I, for one, have reason to be grateful for traditional medical treatments such as antibiotics and surgery. At the same time, I am grateful for Healing Hover Touch—the subject at hand, Healing Touch, Therapeutic Touch, and many other healing disciplines that have been around for many years. Acupuncture, for example, is five thousand-plus years old, and Qigong is three thousand plus years old (and both of them follow the same meridians[1]) Still others are as new as the past forty years, and perhaps some appeared this morning!

In the following pages we shall also explore nutrition and lifestyle as building blocks of a whole and healthy life.

Why This Book Had to Be Written

Often what is written regarding health practices carries with it certain implications. Two are that the author is the author-ity and is the one who can give the greatest amount of help; another is that thoughtful people consider the author's preferred discipline to be the discipline of choice.

Throughout, I will emphasize that not only am I not *the* expert, I am not even *an* expert. I am simply a fellow traveler with a gift. I used this gift unconsciously for several years, at least as far back as my teens. I began to share it consciously with others in 1962. Let me hasten to add that you also have that gift. You may already know that you have it, and you may consciously use it to benefit yourself and others; you may think that everyone can and does use the gift in the same ways you do. You would be right to think that almost everyone has access to the gift of healing; however, not everyone uses it—at least not consciously.

You may even use the gift of healing without being aware that you have it. Some people may be completely unaware of the possibility that their heart, connected to their hands, could ever help another to regain their health.

Neither are Healing Hover Touch, Therapeutic Touch, Reiki, and other similar modalities of treatment the only ways to bring about wholeness. They are, however, a few of the ways health and well-being can be maintained, regained, and sustained. We shall discuss a variety of approaches to healing, a few in some detail, and will at least refer to a wide variety of other exceedingly useful modalities of treatment.

I have observed that the gift of Healing Hover Touch is one that stable adults with whom I have come in contact can use and have used. Many of those contacts have been through television presentations, video distance learning, classes presented personally, in-service trainings, and workshops and learning experiences in hundreds of health-related professional and non-health-related professional settings.

Other contacts have taken place in personal classroom settings where participants learn healing and support behaviors for themselves and loved ones with cancer, multiple sclerosis, broken bones, and other illnesses and injuries. Because television numbers are practically unknowable, I do not know precisely how many have had at least a brief exposure to the subject of this book through my efforts and the efforts of students of Healing Hover Touch. What I do know is that more than 106,000 have learned of it since 1962, including the seven years I practiced but did not yet teach Healing Hover Touch.

I have traveled to all fifty states and to fifty-eight countries on five continents, speaking to health-related professionals and non-professionals, as well as to professional and nonprofessional religious groups in most of them, and I have taught Healing Hover Touch in many of those areas since 1969. So far, I have not met a single adult who is mentally alert who could not identify his personal healing gift to use it to benefit himself and others.

In addition, of those more than 106,000 people who have attended my experiential workshops or classes in person—or by DVD, video, or television—I have often asked the attendees whether or not they have ever had at least one sickness that was truly a benefit to them. Well over twenty thousand people in face-to-face settings have responded to that informal survey. So far, all have indicated that they have had at least one sickness that did enrich them in some way.

Of the more than forty-three thousand face-to-face participants in the class learning experiences, over four thousand are health-care professionals. They include physicians, nurses, chiropractors, veterinarians, reflexologists, massage therapists, and numerous others. Since we have no formal follow-up, I do not know the total numbers who continue to practice. However, some health-care practitioners have made it a point to stay in touch. There are four hundred-plus that I know about who continue to use Healing Hover Touch as one of their modalities of treatment. Of those nonprofessionals who attended primarily to receive help or to help loved ones, over the years I have heard from hundreds who have continued using their new skills to assist friends and family. More than a few have made career changes and have entered one of the many health-care fields. Several have said that this decision was because of what an illness had taught them.

Certainly, not every person felt every illness they had ever had was somehow beneficial. But for those sicknesses that were a benefit, words of thanksgiving are often spoken.

Basically, illness often gives a person a new lease on life, a new view and experience of life. Sometimes that new view may come as a result of a complete healing and recovery of wholeness, and sometimes it comes while they are continuing to experience a chronic or acute illness, or even while they are moving toward death. A kind of paradox occurs when a physical condition from which one does not return to health helps one achieve a newfound wholeness nonetheless.

Paradoxical thinking is creating a big enough container of thoughts so that one can transcend the acceptable norms. In other words, people who are not healed physically, which is the norm, often come to think of themselves as more whole than ever before, exhibiting a new lease on life. While almost all patients strongly desire a return to health and, over a lifetime, most people do regain wholeness repeatedly, it does not always happen. Some people do not regain physical wholeness, but they come to a new understanding of themselves as being well—a realization that is often derived from the crucible of pain and suffering and the reflection precipitated by it.

Much of what we will address in these pages is paradoxical in nature. We will look at numerous relationships and see what healthy and unhealthy ones look like, and how we might improve ours. We will also consider healing that occurred when Healing Hover Touch was utilized after traditional medicine had not worked, and instances when Healing Hover Touch worked in conjunction with traditional or other integrative treatment methods.

Discussion of healing in which traditional and other integrative treatment methods were sometimes successful and sometimes not abounds in other volumes, and we will not focus on that here. We will include physical healings that have not yet occurred, and may never occur, with Hover Touch, traditional medicine, and other integrative treatments of choice. Paradoxical thinking allows for all these possibilities.

Evolution of Medical Terms

Allopathic medicine is a system of therapeutics using medicines and other treatments that produce effects different from those of the disease treated. Allopathy is considered by medical lexicographer and etymologist Taber[2] to be "a term erroneously used for the practice of regular medicine" (i.e., by M.D.s).

Allopathic medicine and medical doctors, however, are inextricably entwined.

Among the first to take the oath of fifth-century BCE Greek physician Hippocrates, the allopath essentially was sworn to do no harm and to observe the healing qualities of nature.

The use of the term *integrative medical treatment* is evidence of evolution in current thinking regarding the way medicine and medical practices are being viewed. Before the term integrative medical treatment was developed, the term of choice was *alternative medicine*; typically, for the past thirty to forty years, all modalities of treatment that were not allopathic medicine (practiced by M.D.s) were placed in the alternative category.

Healing disciplines that fall into the alternative classification include (but are not limited to) chiropractics, acupuncture, acupressure, reflexology, Johrei, Therapeutic Touch, Touch for Health, osteopathy, and massage therapy. Other alternative healing disciplines include Feldenkrais; Rolfing; vitamin, mineral, and herbal therapy; homeopathy; Healing Touch (and non-touch, i.e., Hover); magnetic healing; Kabbalistic healing; deep (Theta) meditation; and laying on of hands. Still others include precautionary dieting, the Optimum Performance Eating Plan (e.g., *Eat Right 4 Your [Blood] Type*, discussed in Chapter 11, "My Experience with Chelation Therapy"), breathing exercises, yoga, physical exercise, pilgrimage to Lourdes, naturopathy, prayer, Reiki, and numerous others. With so many legs under the abundant table of wholeness, we have an excellent foundation and numerous possibilities for healing to occur.

Evidence of rapid change in terms and ways of viewing our evolving world was observed in an oral report in mid-1998 by a friend of mine, the late Dr. David Larson,[3] president of the National Institute for Healthcare Research. Larson indicated that there are 126 medical schools in the United States. In 1994, three medical schools had elective courses in medicine and spiritual healing (with an average enrollment of three to four students).

As of the date of Larson's oral report (just four years later), forty-three medical schools had unitary courses in medicine and spiritual healing, most of which by the year 2000 have become required courses. He also pointed out that most practicing physicians generally prefer the terms *spirituality* and *patient belief* instead of *religion*.

It is interesting to note that many non-medical people with great depths of faith also prefer *spirituality* instead of *religion*.

My intention in this book is not to identify any one term as right or any single way of healing as right, but rather to tune the reader in to the various integrative modalities of treatment that are possible. We will, however, focus on Healing Hover Touch.

As to the term *alternative*, with the passage of time many noticed that the term connoted an *either/or* rather than a *both/and* range of options, which seemed a threat to both patients and allopathic physicians. During the past twenty-plus years, *complementary* medicine began to replace *alternative*, not just to soften the perceived threat that a patient or client must make a choice between allopathic medicine and alternative medicine. In fact, it was largely because most of those in the alternative camps wanted to work *with* allopathic physicians, not to circumvent them.

However *complementary* doesn't appear to be quite appropriate either, and it is increasingly being replaced with *integrative*. *Complementary* left one with the feeling that any discipline that was not allopathic was an also-ran; it existed only on the fringes as a feel-good extra. A new name was needed.

If Andrew Weil (a Harvard-trained M.D. with an undergraduate degree in botany) did not invent the term *integrative medicine,* he surely is one of the chief proponents for its use. Weil is editor-in-chief of a peer-reviewed scientific journal, *Integrative Medicine*, which is highlighted in the newsletter *Self Healing*.[4]

Integrative medicine is a term I happily support using. For me, it is not just a term to add to one's vocabulary; it is a way of thinking, breathing, feeling, behaving, and being. The client/patient will usually need to proactively seek on her own initiative secondary or tertiary modalities (or integrative), since few health practitioners will encourage seeking health practices that are different from their own.

Throughout the 1990s, many advocates of alternative medicine increasingly used the term *integrative medicine*, and now they often use it interchangeably with *integrative modalities of treatment* and *integrative medical treatment*. At least for now, *integrative medicine* seems the most consistently used term, although some modalities of treatment are not medicine/medical as these terms are generally used.

For example, Asian Qigong masters, who may also be Chinese medical doctors, speak of balancing a patient's energy with their hands, usually without actually touching the patient (external Qigong).[5] What the patient generally learns to do for himself in breathing exercises, physical movement, visualization, or meditation is internal Qigong. For an excellent Qigong volume of breathing and physical exercises, active meditations, and diet, see

Cohen's book, *The Way of Qigong: The Art and Science of Chinese Energy Healing.*[6]

Integrative modalities of treatment is often the term of choice for devotees of alternative medicine and at times is the most precise term as well. It is my term of choice and, unless otherwise noted, is the elongated term being referred to when I use *integrative* throughout the book. I see the four terms—allopathic, alternative, complementary, and integrative—and the treatment disciplines they represent as so interwoven that health-care professionals and their patients should be able to pick and choose at will the best modality(ties) for any given physical condition. Healing Hover Touch is among those disciplines that fall into the integrative modalities of treatment.

CHAPTER TWO

What Migraines, Biofeedback, and Healing Hover Touch Have in Common

Medical and prayer researcher Larry Dossey, M.D. is a friend with whom I have served for several years on the John Templeton Foundation's Humility Theology Information Center Advisory Board. You may be familiar with Dr. Dossey's published research. He told me in 1997[7] that as a young physician he intended to be a surgeon and that during his residency he frequently experienced severe migraine headaches.

Dr. Dossey was dealing with the possibility that he might need to go into some other kind of medicine. The chief surgeon on staff at the hospital had read about biofeedback and suggested that Dossey try it. This procedure is based on a discovery that if a person learned to warm his hands through mental focus, there was a positive effect on blood flow in the brain. Dossey tried biofeedback training, and it worked. His migraine headaches were cured.

With biofeedback equipment, the galvanic skin response (GSR) confirms that if you concentrate, you can make your fingers and your hands warmer. What happens in the hands also happens in the head. The migraine headache is "thought to be the result of vasodilation of extracerebral cranial arteries."[7] They constrict to a point where either very little or no blood can get through, and then there is enough dilation that there is mild relief. When you learn to consciously warm your hands, that same warming mechanism goes on in the brain. Essentially, Dossey taught himself not to have migraine headaches. (For other ways to prevent headaches, see the "Nutrition, Breathing, Physical Exercises, and Meditation in Health and Well-Being" section in Chapter 12.)

Three Eras of Western Medicine

Dossey[8] also identified three critical epochs in the development of Western medicine during the last 140-plus years. He calls them Era I, Era II, and Era III medicine.

Era I medicine has been developing in the Western world approximately since the 1860s, the decade of the American Civil War; it is the world of anesthesia and surgery. This is a beginning stage of sophisticated medicine in the West. (My own great-great-uncle is part of that world. He developed anesthesia, for which he was knighted. Sir James Young Simpson was a Scotsman and, for his development of anesthesia, a huge memorial to him has been erected on the front lawn of Edinburgh Castle.) Europe, North America, and South America are parts of the Western world where Era I medicine has been developing.

Although the idea that the mind and body interact is an ancient one, it began to impact Era I medicine only after World War II. Eventually, Era I and II approaches began cooperating with one another.

Era II medicine acknowledges that your mind can affect your body, and that *your* mind can affect *my* body, and vice versa. The Eastern world has known this for millennia; the Western world has been aware of some of the possibilities since the mid-1800s, as was marked by the early developments of hypnosis in the West. It was the mid-1900s before the West began making practical use not just of hypnosis but also of the fact that your mind can affect my body in other ways as well.

Physicians in China are not considered to be legitimate physicians if they have not been graduated from two medical schools:

the old Chinese medical school, which teaches ways to mix and prescribe eight hundred-plus herbs, and a modern medical school, which teaches the use of the antibiotics and surgery of the Western world.

Since Era III medicine is important, but is not the primary era in which Healing Hover Touch falls, I will discuss Era III briefly in Chapter 3, "How Healing Hover Touch Works."

Using Healing Hover Touch

Era II medicine is the one with which Healing Hover Touch is most related. We acknowledge a mind-body connection and that your mind can affect my body and my mind can affect yours. Healing Touch, Therapeutic Touch, and Healing Hover Touch practitioners add the ingredients of the heart and hands. Your mind can affect my body through connecting your mind, your heart, and your hands. And vice versa. Generally, Era II medicine requires that the practitioner and the client are relatively close to each other.

When I began using Healing Hover Touch with clients in hospitals in 1962, medical personnel watched me suspiciously. Since the early 1980s—when I would offer to step aside and resume when the medical practitioner was finished—nurses, physicians, and physical therapists have asked me to continue and if they could watch. We've come a long way, but there's still a long way to go.

Much of this needed progress has to do with the way we ask to be able to help others and the intention of our hearts. We begin by knowing that God does not *have* anything that we need, but that God *is* everything that we need.

Mosley and Hill observed that there appears to be an almost universal awareness that in our times of greatest need or of greatest joy, humankind calls out for help or to express gratitude. But who or what are we calling out to, and are we being heard?

They continue by saying that the eighteenth-century Swedish visionary, scientist, and theologian Emanuel Swedenborg "wrote that God already knows what we need, but we must go through the step of asking for it. God hears all prayers and looks only to the heart of the person praying to know the sincerity or appropriateness of the plea. If we want our prayers to be answered, we need to look within ourselves to sense the purity of our heart's request."[9]

Let me add that seeking to develop your Healing Hover Touch skills through prayer and practice is not only to affect the physical body of another positively. The use of one's hands and good intentions to influence another's well-being may also include higher emotional, mental, and spiritual health as well.

Migraines Healed

It is this exchange of energy that we repeatedly see and experience in the Healing Hover Touch interactive learning experiences and practice. The following firsthand account deals with a twelve-year migraine in a different way. The sufferer would have five minutes of relief at a time periodically through a twenty-four-hour day.

Periodically, someone who has had a dramatic healing in one learning experience will attend a subsequent learning experience and tell her story. I asked Joan to share her experience. The following is a summary of her testimonial to an assembly of several hundred physicians, patients, clergy, and laypersons.

> Good evening. It is a pleasure to be here. This is a surprise, but it is a wonderful surprise. Last fall we had a retreat in my hometown, and Glenn asked if there was anyone in the audience who had a headache. I volunteered because I had been carrying a headache around for quite a few years; I had migraines for at least twelve years. I can't explain to you what happened, but I can say it was through my belief and my accepting that my healing did occur. I thank God for whatever happened, and I don't know exactly what happened, but I did believe it. I can stand here and say that I feel wonderful. I don't even have them [migraines] anymore. Believe it and accept it, and you, too, can receive your healing through love.

There are a couple points to be made regarding what Joan said about believing and love. First, she said that she was healed through the power of her belief. For her I think that is true.

However, many skeptics and outright nonbelievers have also been healed. Sometimes people come to prove that there is nothing valid about Healing Hover Touch.

One such woman was a physician from England. She and her husband had come to a learning experience I was facilitating in Mexico in 1998. Actually, she came at her husband's urging and volunteered to be my first demonstration model; this was before I asked participants to choose a partner with whom to practice. She had had migraine headaches almost nonstop for seventeen years. In addition, she also had had severe lower back pain for nearly that same length of time.

We were less than three minutes into the treatment when she began sobbing uncontrollably. In the midst of tears, she said, "I have no pain, I have no pain, I have no pain!" Later, when she was more composed, she asked for the microphone. What she told registrants from thirty-four countries was that she had agreed to attend this particular session instead of another because of her husband's insistence and to get him to quit nagging her. She had come to prove this was a hoax, however well-intentioned it was.

Finally, she looked at me and said, "This was the most real healing experience of my life with me as either the practitioner or the recipient. I plan to pay very close attention for the balance of this workshop, because you can believe I will add it to what I can do to help people." (I have had similar responses from veterinarians, nurses, and numerous types of health practitioners who have been looking for another way to be of help.)

So, these two women, Joan and the physician, came with two different mind-sets; they had two different experiences but with the same end result: both were healed. All the physician needed to do was be willing to go through the behaviors that allowed her to receive a treatment; she did not need to believe that it would make a difference. Benson[10] makes the same point: that certain behaviors will trigger the relaxation response, "whether or not you believe that it will." The point could be made in the case of the English physician, that her *desire* to be healed, although different from *belief*, might have been equal in importance to belief.

Joan encouraged people to come be healed through love. Joan's last phrase, "can receive your healing through love," is the one I want to speak to because that is what happens. Participants often ask, "What do you do mentally when you place your hands in front of the client's face? What are you doing?" With a smile, I say that I'm doing something very scientific. It is really not difficult. I am setting my intention that the very highest good may be manifest in the client's life and affairs and—at least silently—I say "I love you."

That is so much a part of what it takes to be able to help. As a practitioner, you set your intention of good and you send love to the client. Your mind sets the intention, your heart sends love, and both are projected through your hands. What happens is that you begin to affect and influence the other person's energy.

When Joan volunteered, I was asking only for a common headache, not a migraine that had debilitated her for twelve years. When Joan responded, she immediately started crying. Her headache disappeared more quickly than any common two-hour headache I had ever seen. Joan's doctor, who was sitting in the front row, confirmed that she had had frequent and severe headaches for twelve years.

Sensing Through a Person's Aura

A person's aura is thought of as a surrounding, distinctive, but intangible, essence—or an atmosphere. A very few people seem to see the auras of all, or most, others and describe it in terms of colors or light. Still others appear to be able to see the auras of only a few people, and some can see only a few people's auras only occasionally. Most people appear not to see auras at all. Perhaps everyone could learn to see auras, perhaps not.

With the advent of Kirlian photography, it is now possible to see the colors of light emanating from both people and inanimate objects. The pictures of a human being often resemble a person standing in a furnace of flames.

Normally, I cannot see the auras of people. But it appears to me that I can and do *feel* their auras. It also appears that that is the sensation field—also called warmth, energy, body energy, Qi (pronounced *chee*), heat, tingling, intense tingling, etc.—that is experienced by healing touch and non-touch practitioners, Qigong masters, and others who practice hands-on caregiving.

It appears that when the practitioner feels a cool spot, they have discovered a rupture in the aura. That same spot often has no extraordinary sensation at all to the client or, if it does, it may feel hot instead of cold. It seems reasonable that an infection would feel hot to the client, because the body energy focuses on the infection to deal with it.

Not all changes in temperature feel cool or cold to the practitioner's hands; some of the changes feel warm or hot. For example, a rise in body temperature can occur in the right lower back if the liver is diseased. As is mentioned elsewhere, if the face and head are congested, they will often feel several degrees warmer to the practitioner than the rest of the body. However, a rupture, or what appears to be a gap or hole in the aura, will generally effect a perceptible lowering of temperature at the point of the rupture; occasionally, with some people, the temperature may rise.

The human skin is the largest organ *of* the body (the liver is the largest organ *in* the body), and it is the organ that sloughs off both toxins in the body and some of the body's own wastes. When the pores of the skin get plugged up, the body energy that would normally be directed outward is necessarily redirected inward.

The balancing of body energy is an effort to reignite the energy normally associated with the cold (or hot) spot. The practitioner-healer moves the hands around in a clockwise fashion, and then counterclockwise (either direction first—it makes no difference), and finally up and down and from side to side in front of the spot. Actually, not only the body energy of the practitioner is being utilized: The circular motion begins in a larger circle around the cold (or hot) spot so that the practitioner picks up some of the client's positive energy. Then the practitioner's hands move into smaller circles to use the positive energy as a kind of pilot light to transform the negative energy field that appears as a cold (or occasionally a hot) spot.

Whether the spot is hot or cold, the practitioner-healer works to normalize the temperature, and the tissues beneath the spot are also being normalized.

Exchange of Energy

An extensive energy exchange often takes place between the practitioner and the client. Borysenko[11] reported on the work of Therapeutic Touch researcher Janet Quinn (who has a Ph.D. in nursing). Borysenko says that a nurse first thinks of the person with whom she is working with the greatest respect and as a whole and healthy person. Next, while she is doing Therapeutic Touch with her hands (not physically touching, but touching the energy field), she can raise the T-lymphocyte function in the recipient. There is an equal rise in the same function in the nurse who gives the treatment.

The balancing of body energy treatment is good for self-healing as well; somehow it seems easier if someone with an interest in Healing Hover Touch is available with whom to share it. However, I do practice self-healing if no one is around who can do it for me. In the past, when the weather changed from day to day, I sometimes would get a sinus pressure headache, especially with the change of the seasons. Upon awakening with a season-change headache, while still lying in bed, I have taken the hand of my sleeping wife (Martha) and placed it directly over the bridge of my nose and forehead. I leave it there for awhile, and the headache disappears. I do not believe this experience nullifies the belief that good intentions from practitioner to client are needed; in fact, I believe that even while she is asleep, Martha still loves me and has good intentions towards me.

The Ingredient of Intention

A key ingredient of healing is the practitioner having good intentions for, caring for, or loving the client. And often the client is not in a class or in an office as a result of a planned appointment. Sometimes healing encounters simply happen where they happen. Because she wrote me and gave me permission to use her name, I will let Becky Norman (real name) tell her story through her letter:

> It was a warm summer evening and I had been suffering with a headache for a week. I work for a chiropractor and usually get adjustments to relieve my headaches, but this time that just wasn't working. It was a continuous pain towards the top of my head that would not quit no matter what I did.
>
> Glenn came into my office and I was telling him about this headache. He said that he knew something he could try that would make my headache go away. I stood in the middle of the room and Glenn started his work. All of a sudden, I was sweating and felt sick to my stomach. It was as if I could actually feel him drawing something out from my body. We then went outside so I could get some fresh air, and when I was ready we continued. By the time Glenn was finished, my headache was gone. He drew the pain right out of my head and never even touched me! Since that time, I have had headaches off and on but not anything like that one was.

How Healing Hover Touch Works

The following is a transcript of a healing that occurred during a three-hour interactive learning experience. The commentary provided is explanatory information for the participants who were observing the healing demonstration.

———(o)———

The reason that I often choose a headache as an example is so that I won't take too much time from facilitating a complete learning experience. If I do this in a counseling session or a healing session, either in my office or in a small class, then I can work with everybody one-on-one at some point. I will demonstrate the headache healing technique and then we shall continue with the other ways we practice Healing Hover Touch. Anything that happens with a headache can happen with tumors—and has.

People who have had heart attacks and were scheduled for four-way bypasses the next day have had their surgery delayed because their blood count changed. Doctors did not know what was wrong at first, and then they began to realize there was something right going on. Two or three days later, the patients went home with no detectable muscle damage to their hearts remaining. That has happened a few times over the years; it is not just one exceptional case.

At times I am the practitioner, and other times I receive calls from people who were my students, functioning as practitioners. They tell me that a major healing happened to a client or patient of theirs. (Unless you are a licensed medical practitioner, you are called the practitioner and the person you work with is your client, not your patient.)

Typical Headache Healing with Teresa

Glenn: Does anyone have a two-hour headache?

Teresa: Yes.

Glenn: Have we ever seen each other before?

Teresa: No. This is my first time here.

Glenn: Well, welcome, Teresa. Where is the headache?

Teresa: Behind my right eye.

Glenn: Where is it now? [Glenn did not do anything; he was only checking to see if a change had already taken place.]

Teresa: It is still there.

Glenn: That's fine. Now, I am going to put my hands in front of your face briefly, and what I am going to be looking for is a heat or energy level. Close your eyes, take a deep breath, and hold. Breathe out just as deeply. Again, breathe in very deeply, hold, and breathe out just as deeply. And again, breathe in very deeply, hold, and out just as deeply. Resume breathing normally, and continue to relax. This breathing exercise is part of Teresa's internal Qigong. This is what she is doing for herself.

What I am going to do is external Qigong—external to her—and this is Healing Hover Touch. I do not actually touch without asking if I may. I may tell the client where I want to touch them and ask if that is all right. Right now [with hands in front of Teresa's face], I am feeling for energy to see what her face feels like, because that is what the rest of her body most likely will feel like. There can be a change in temperature. Normal indoor clothing is just fine to wear during an assessment, although it is better not to wear a coat or heavy sweater. As you practice and develop your Healing Hover Touch skills, generally you will begin to feel the heat or coolness that is present. [To Teresa] Close your eyes. May I place my index and middle fingers on your forehead, above your eyes?

Teresa: Yes.

Glenn: The reason I do that is because people concentrate better when they have fingers up here, either their own or mine. Visualize Rodin's famous sculpture *The Thinker* for a moment, with his head resting lightly on the back of his closed hand, reflecting.

Have you ever taken an examination and sat with your head in your hand while you wrote with the other hand? That is because we instinctively know that if we put our hands here [Glenn puts his hand on his own forehead], we are literally exciting what Easterners call—and what increasing numbers of Westerners recognize as—the third or inner eye, a part of our interior or internal Qigong. We activate the third or inner eye and remember things we have no other way of remembering.

I am going to ask Teresa not to point to where the headache is, but to tell me. My fingers are above her eyes. I am going to ask Teresa to locate the pain orally, so that she can really own this headache. If the client only points to the pain, it is highly unlikely the pain is at the skin surface level, which is the only place one can point to.

Glenn: Tell me where it is now.

Teresa: Part of my eye, toward the inside.

Glenn: Toward the front of the right eye. Okay. What color is the pain?

Teresa: Green. It's green.

Glenn: What size is the pain? Big as a barn? Small as a house? A baseball?

Teresa: A baseball, but it's gone down to a golf ball.

Glenn: What color is the pain?

Teresa: It's green and it has some black in it.

Glenn: Green with some black. Where is the pain?

Teresa: The same area.

Glenn: No, please don't tell me "the same area"; tell me where.

Teresa: Inside my eye toward my nose.

Glenn: Inside toward the nose. Has that shifted?

Teresa: Yes, it has.

Glenn: It has shifted. Where is the pain now?

Teresa: Toward the internal rectus of my right eye.

Glenn: Are you a physician or nurse?

Teresa: No.

Glenn: All right, the internal rectus [one of four short muscles of the eye] of the right eye.

Teresa: I had surgery when I was a child.

Glenn: I see. Okay. What color is the pain?

Teresa: Some white and some yellow... more white.

Glenn: How big is the pain?

Teresa: About the size of a marble.

Glenn: It's about the size of a marble. Do you want to let it go?

Teresa: Yes.

Glenn: Are you sure?

Teresa: Yes.

Glenn: Absolutely positive that you want to release it?

Teresa: Yes.

Glenn: Is there a payoff for keeping it?

Teresa: Not that I can see.

Glenn: Not that you can see. So you really want to let it go?

Teresa: Yes, I do.

Glenn: Now?

Teresa: Yes.

Glenn: OK. On the count of three, it rises up and goes out through the crown chakra. The crown chakra is on top of the head—the soft spot on the head of an infant. It's not soft on an adult, but the crown chakra is where most of the heat rises and goes out from the body, and so can the energy of pain. But more important than just the releasing of the pain are all of the causes of the pain. The pain and its cause come together like congealed energy, like a large ball of energy that gets smaller, smaller, smaller until it is the size of a small green pea that is soft like cotton candy (not hard like a green pea).The green pea is soft like cotton candy that would dissolve in the rain. Now, it rises up and goes out through the crown chakra on the count of three. Going up, one . . . up, two . . . up, three [snaps fingers]. And, it's gone, paradoxically.

Teresa: It's gone.

Working with Paradox

We are conducting a metaphysical witch hunt when we ask, "Why did I do this to myself? What happened? Who caused this? What did I do? What's wrong with me?"

None of that matters. Think paradoxically.

Paradoxical thinking allows us to realize that it is not necessary to blame oneself or others for an illness. Neither is it necessary to categorize a sickness as good or bad. Sometimes there are identifiable reasons for a sickness; sometimes there are not. Part of the time, the client is primarily responsible for the sickness; sometimes he is not.

Paradoxical thinking doesn't require that, as a prerequisite to healing, the patient be right or wrong, responsible or not, for the sickness. Finding someone, including one's self, or something to blame only deters one from the task at hand: beginning to do something constructive about the sickness. Be gentle with yourself whether you are the practitioner or the client of Healing Hover Touch. Do not push. We cannot force healings to occur, nor can we force our natural growth in developing our Healing Hover Touch skills. We can practice and remain open to a natural development from within, but we cannot force the development.

Let's return to the healing with Teresa for a moment. Occasionally someone will say, "That's just hypnosis." That is not accurate, but what difference would it make if it were true? What *is* true is that I was directing love and the intention that Teresa's highest good might be manifest in her body, life, and affairs. Teresa's contribution included deep breathing and relaxing: internal Qigong. My contribution was the balancing of body energy with my heart and hands: external Qigong.

When I shake hands with a person with whom I am going to

Thoughts on Forgiveness

For health to flow freely (like water in a pipe), the mind-body vessel needs to be free of debris. Either recent anger or long-term resentment can continue to do or begin to do bodily harm. Every major religion[12] and many—if not most—medical researchers and researchers in psychotherapy[13] insist that forgiveness is necessary to mind-body health.

Those involved with Alcoholics Anonymous may know a book entitled *The Sermon on the Mount*, by Emmet Fox. This small book, with big contents, was AA's first "Big Book." The following exercise derives from principles of forgiveness that were outlined by Fox.[14]

You need to be *willing* to forgive yourself and others.

In order to identify those you may need to forgive, take a brief heart check. Do you rehearse run-ins with people? Do you wish you had said or done something differently, of either a more or less hurtful nature? Do you keep those memories close to your breast, to keep them warm and alive? The people you need to forgive are the people in these memories.

Seek a place where you can be alone and quiet.

Seated, close your eyes and imagine the person you are about to forgive as though he or she was sitting before you.

Then you may quietly say, "I fully and freely forgive X" (saying the person's name). Then claim freedom from the past offense for the other person and for yourself. Envision good life experiences for the other person—whatever that person would see for himself or herself.

Observe how resentments disappear; the effect on your happiness, your bodily health, and your general life experience will be nothing less than revolutionary.

practice Healing Hover Touch, the treatment has already started. There are times when just greeting the client begins the immediate projection of a deeply caring energy. The client may come to you for a specific reason, or she may be a family member who you realize has a pain or other physical problem, and you may offer to help.

Healing with Children

As she was growing up, one of my daughters, Susan, would occasionally come to me for a healing treatment. Her first serious Healing Hover Touch treatment came when she was about nine months old. We lived on Long Island in New York, and we had just had a huge snow dump—as it's referred to in Alaska—of something like twenty inches in nonstop storming in just over twenty-four hours. Nothing was moving, and Susan became ill and developed a fever that continued to rise. The first sign that she was sick was that she did not want to get down on the floor to play with her brother, Buddy (as he was called then), and sister, Tracey.

We called the children's pediatrician and the hospital emergency room for advice. The neighborhood pharmacy I could have walked to was closed because the pharmacist couldn't get to his store. We were not prepared for this kind of emergency.

Tracey had taken the last of the children's aspirin less than a week before, so we didn't even have that available. The fever continued to climb until it was 104 degrees. I took Susan in my arms and sat down in a big easy chair and tried to cover as much of her as I could with my arms and chest. She was totally limp in my arms. I just held her and told her aloud over and over that I loved her. Silently, I visualized her forehead—which most of the time I covered with my hand—and her whole body beginning to cool. I had only begun using my hands consciously in this way about the time of Susan's birth nine months before. It was another couple of years before I gave the practice a name.

When I had held her about two to three hours, she pushed herself far enough away from my chest so she could look at my eyes. Susan began talking when she was fourteen months old, so she did not use words at this moment, but I remember exactly what I thought that look was saying: "I know what you're doing." She laid her little, unusually pink face back on my chest.

In about thirty minutes more, she began to perspire. In fact, we both did. After a half hour more of perspiring, we changed all of her clothes and my shirt. Less than an hour later, the first effort she made to leave my arms was to get down onto the floor to play with Buddy and Tracey. She was too weak to play for long, but her temperature was down to 99.

Something I have noticed through the years since then is that small children and household pets seem to respond positively very quickly, perhaps because they just trust and accept so readily. Ironically to me, during my early years I had intended to be a physician. During my mid-teens, I was even more specific, thinking about possibly becoming a pediatrician or a veterinarian.

Like me, in her youth, Susan often had change-of-season, sometimes debilitating, sinus headaches. As a teen, Susan good-naturedly referred to my healing-hands practices as "voodoo." Recently, I visited Susan and her family in Delaware; the weather was changing drastically. She came into the room where I was talking with her son and daughter and stuck out her face as she had often done as a teenager and said, "Dad, do your voodoo."

On that particular occasion, I only passed one hand over her face and said, "That really *is* a bad pain, *wasn't* it?"

With the pain instantly gone, she smiled and said, "That still always amazes me."

Lest you conclude that her *expectation* of feeling better or of having a headache completely disappear in an instant was why it happened so fast, read on.

Hover Touch in Passing

One time during my travels, I was changing airplanes in Chicago; I was pulling one piece of luggage with a computer attached to it with my right hand. As I approached the main terminal, where I needed to change directions to catch my second plane, two skycaps standing on opposite sides of the corridor appeared to be taking a work break. At that moment, few people were in the corridor. Still, those skycaps had to raise their voices to hear each other. One asked the other if he had any aspirin because he had what he referred to as a "hammering headache." The second man indicated that he did not have any pain medication.

As I approached the two men, but before I was actually next to them, I asked, "If I promise not to touch you, but I eliminate the headache, is that all right with you?"

"Yes, man, it's all right."

As I passed him, I passed my free hand over his face and said the same thing I had to Susan at her home: "That really *is* a bad pain, *wasn't* it?" I never completely stopped walking.

As I moved on down the corridor, he yelled to me, "Hey, man, what did you do?"

I yelled back, "Is the pain gone?" When he said it was, I bid him a good day.

Who Can Use This Technique?

So by now, you may be asking whether you can effectively practice Healing Hover Touch. There is much that says you can. Three criteria seem to be necessary to practice Healing Hover Touch successfully.

First, you must remember to breathe. Remain relaxed, be of good humor, and *breathe!* Follow the principles in this book and practice with someone else, and you can teach another person to be a practitioner for you.

Second, you need to have an interest in doing this type of healing.

To evaluate the third criterion, place the palms of your hands facing one another in front of you about eighteen to twenty inches apart. Move the palms toward each other slowly, but do not allow them to touch. Continue moving your hands toward each other until they are about an inch apart, and then stop. What kinds of sensations, if any, do you feel? It is all right if you don't feel anything on the first try. The first time, you may not feel anything special or different.

Try moving your hands in circular motions in opposite directions, palms facing each other and still an inch apart. Sometimes when you move the hands in a circular motion, you begin to feel something, even if you did not just a minute before.

What does that feel like? Vibrations? Tingling? Energy? Heat? Magnetic heat? Needles? None of those answers is wrong. They are all right. What you feel is what you feel. Feeling those sensations is the third evidence that you can provide Healing Hover Touch to others.

Personally, I experience the energy in a variety of ways; sometimes my hands feel tingly. The more you practice feeling the sensations in your hands, the greater the variety of sensations you are likely to experience. My hands often have such a tingling sensation that it as though there are hundreds of needles in each hand. Often, the tingling is intense. Actually, it is quite a pleasant sensation. It feels very sharp and prickly, but nice and warm, and no pain is involved. Often, the client on the receiving end of that energy acknowledges that is what she is feeling also—a pleasant warmth. Clients, totally unprompted, will even describe the tingly needles and other sensations being experienced by the practitioner.

About the Warm or Cool Spots of a Client

Some practitioners of energy bodywork say that when they feel a change in temperature somewhere on the client's body, it is cool or cold. Others say that the change is warm or hot. Still other practitioners feel that the two ends of the continuum seem to change from client to client. I believe all of the above are not only possible, but true.

However, the sensation may be related to the practitioner as well. It is possible that one practitioner's hands get extremely warm so that, even if the client has an elevated temperature anywhere on the body, that spot still might feel cool to the therapist. However, it will feel warmer than the rest of the client's body.

Conversely, another therapist, just as perceptive and capable as the first one, may find that her hand temperature does not rise much, or may even find that the temperature is lowered during a treatment. For this practitioner, then, a feverish spot on a client might seem quite warm.

When I began, late in the 1960s, to facilitate classes on Healing

Hover Touch, I told students that the spots would be cool. Except for head and face infections, which appeared warm to me, all other spots that changed in temperature almost always showed up as cool to me. Over time, I had students who were doing very well with the system, but they shared that the spots that felt cool to me felt warm to them. I accept both phenomena at face value.

What We Don't Know

It seems to me that the human energy field (HEF) practitioners don't know *how* Healing Touch, Therapeutic Touch, or Healing Hover Touch works. We only know that they *do*. The same is true of Qigong in China. The Chinese only began trying to study Qigong in 1978[1], and they continue to attempt to create more experiments to increase their understanding of it. They, too, know it works; they are seeking a better understanding of how.

In December 2000, the news media announced that in 2001 a new regulation would go into effect: that physicians must treat a patient's pain on its own account and not just as a side effect. It was reported that there is evidence that when a patient is not in pain, he begins to heal more quickly.

I don't pretend to know how pain is eased through Healing Hover Touch, Therapeutic Touch, and Healing Touch so quickly and effectively, but I've witnessed it many hundreds of times. It would be an oversimplification to assume that all healings follow the same pattern, but is it possible that these three systems effect many healings by first causing the pain to subside, and the healing then follows?

Two Additional Healing Hover Touch Sessions

During a national convention learning experience, I asked if anyone in the room had an ache, pain, or condition that was not a headache that they were willing to share with the group for a demonstration.

Sometimes, when the client is clearly in pain and knows exactly where it is located, I delay the balancing of body energy (see Chapter 4, items 5 through 21). Instead, I move directly to the deep breathing with my hands in front of the face, or my two fingers touching the forehead just above the eyebrows.

The first volunteer, Gene, was clearly one of those who needed pain relief in the left side of his neck, shoulder, and all down the left side of his body.

Glenn: Are you willing to release the pain and the cause of the pain, including forgiving yourself and others if necessary? [Sometimes I ask this or a similar question early in the treatment, and sometimes I do it after the assessment or even after the balancing of energy. The part of the question about forgiving is something I usually do spontaneously and intuitively; therefore, I do not ask that of everyone.]

Gene: Yes, I am.

Glenn: [To Gene] Is it all right if I put my fingers on your forehead above your eyes?

Gene: It's all right.

Glenn: Take a deep breath—a really deep breath—in, hold it, and then breathe out just as deeply. And a second time, breathe in very deeply, hold it, and exhale through the mouth, very deeply and slowly. And a third time, breathe in very deeply, hold it, and breathe out just as deeply and slowly. Okay, resume breathing normally, and continue to relax. Feeling very calm and serene. Where is the pain, Gene? Don't point; tell me instead.

Gene: Left neck to the shoulder.

Glenn: Okay, what color is the pain?

Gene: It had a yellow look when you said that.

Glenn: What color is it now?

Gene: Kind of a dark red.

Glenn: That's a good color. How big is it? As big as a barn?

A garage? A house? A baseball?

Gene: It's as big as my whole left side.

Glenn: Okay, where is it now? If it's in the same place, don't tell me "the same place"—just describe it again. Where is the pain?

Gene: In my left shoulder.

Glenn: Okay, not at the neck? What color is it now?

Gene: I don't get a color. Just black.

Glenn: Gone from red to black, right?

Gene: Yes.

Glenn: Okay, how big is the pain?

Gene: It is less.

Glenn: Okay, that is progress. What color is it now?

Gene: A bright green up above. It's still dark below.

Glenn: Okay, where is the pain now?

Gene: Still in my left shoulder.

Glenn: How big is it?

Gene: About half what it was.

Glenn: What color is it?

Gene: Red and black.

Glenn: Are you ready to let it go?

Gene: Yes.

Glenn: You're sure you don't have any payoff for keeping it?

Gene: No.

Glenn: That means you are really ready to let it go?

Gene: I'm ready.

Glenn: You're not getting Josie [Gene's wife] to do things for you that you would have to do yourself if you didn't have the pain?

Gene: No.

Glenn: Okay. We just image the pain and the cause of the pain. Sometimes, looking for the cause of the pain is a metaphysical witch hunt. You don't really need to know what caused it, because the infinite intelligence that helps you relieve it can also tell you how to avoid the pain and its cause in the future.

So we just envision that the pain and the cause of the pain are coming together as a congealed ball of energy. It gets smaller, smaller, smaller, and reduces in size until it is the size of a small green pea. It is soft like cotton candy that would dissolve in the rain. This is the crown chakra up here [pointing to the top of the head]—what we call the soft spot on the head of an infant. It is not soft on an adult, but the spot is still there. It is where a great deal of our energy is released, both positive and negative. Sometimes, men think of it as heat loss, especially if they don't have much hair up there to stop the loss of heat. Okay, so that is where that ball of energy is going out. It is emanating from the body through the crown chakra. That is where we want the pain to exit.

First, it reduces in size. It is the size of a small green pea, like cotton candy that would dissolve in the rain. It rises up and goes out through the crown chakra on the count of three. Going up ... one. Going up ... two. Going up ... three, and it is gone. Now, where is the pain?

Gene: Seems to be gone.

33

Glenn: Let's check to see if we have eliminated pain in the neck, shoulder, and side joints. Keep your feet where they are, and turn to the right just a little bit. Just leave your feet where they are. Okay, make any difference? Any pain?

Gene: No.

Glenn: Okay, go back to the left. All right? Now, how are you?

Gene: Much better.

[A second volunteer who came up at the same time as Gene was Sheila. Sheila had a severe neck injury.]

Glenn: Close your eyes; relax your arms. Just relax. Are you willing to release the pain and injury? Or do you have a payoff for keeping the pain? [I will come back with a fuller explanation of this line of questioning, which I use with most everyone, at the conclusion of the healing work with Sheila.]

Sheila: Yes.

Glenn: May I place my fingertips on your forehead above your eyes?

Sheila: Yes.

Glenn: Okay, tell me where the pain is. Don't point; just describe it.

Sheila: Back of the neck.

Glenn: What color is the pain?

Sheila: Gray.

Glenn: How big is it? Big as a barn?

Sheila: Yes, big as a barn.

Glenn: You do things in a big way! Where is it now?

Sheila:	Left side of the neck, a little bit.
Glenn:	What color is it?
Sheila:	It's a light blue.
Glenn:	How big is it?
Sheila:	Like an orange.
Glenn:	No longer a barn. It is an orange?
Sheila:	Yes.
Glenn:	Where is the pain right now?
Sheila:	Can't feel it now.
Glenn:	Don't feel it now?
Sheila:	No.
Glenn:	Keep your feet planted where they are. Let's turn just a little bit; only in this case, turn your head instead of your whole body. How is that? No pain?
Sheila:	No.
Glenn:	Okay, turn the other way. How is that?
Sheila:	Good.
Glenn:	Finished?
Sheila:	Finished.

Does the Client Really Want Healing?

As was promised above, here is a fuller explanation for the line of questions, "Are you ready to let this pain or condition go? Is there a payoff for keeping it?" When the client responds with a "Yes" to the first question or a "No" to the second question and there appears to be little or no thought behind the answer, I will ask again, sometimes differently. I may ask, "Does having the condition or pain allow you to control others or allow you to get out of fulfilling responsibilities you might otherwise have to fulfill?"

Sometimes the answer is "No," and they walk away in a class; or people in my office say that they want to think about it; or they answer, "Not now." Answers such as those are—or have already been—well thought through. People usually get well—and much more quickly—if they *want* to get well.

I made the above point at the 1998 national conference of the American Academy of Family Physicians. Two women physicians—partners in a family care practice—were practice partners during my presentation. At discussion time, one of them said, "I have always wanted to ask some of my patients if they really wanted to get well, and now I will ask that when I feel inclined. There are patients you just feel are wasting your time and theirs, and their insurance company's money. I realize some are lonely or are looking for attention, but perhaps this line of questioning can help them determine what they really want."

Additional Details of These Healing Demonstrations

Refer back to the healings described above. Notice that with Gene, I asked him to take three deep breaths, to hold, and to exhale deeply after each breath, before I asked the location, color, and size of the pain. With Sheila, I suggested only that she relax with her arms at her sides. I placed my fingertips on her forehead just above her eyes so that she could concentrate deeply when I asked her about the location, color, and size of the pain.

Both Gene and Sheila were in severe pain, so I worked to free them of the pain first. Also, in both cases, in a further effort to effect a healing after the pain had ceased, I went back and did a complete balancing of body energy (see the instructions in Chapter 4).

Using Physical Touch in a Healing

If you, the reader, are going to do a Healing Hover Touch treatment and you decide you need to touch the client, ask the client if she is comfortable with physical touch. I've never had anybody say "No." For one thing, sometimes the client says "Yes" out of curiosity. The client wants to see what you do.

Sometimes during a Healing Hover Touch procedure, I may spontaneously decide that I want to *actually* touch the client, and I may ask for that permission again even if I asked at the beginning of the session. I tell him where I want to touch him; sometimes I don't have any idea for how long until I'm doing it. It is usually a matter of thirty seconds to five minutes. Oftentimes when that is the case, it is when I am working on a joint. I may sense the need to hold a bone or a joint pretty firmly, and, in fact, I may press fairly hard. I often say to the client, "I really want to press on this area; I want to press firmly. If this begins to hurt you, let me know."

So far, people have said, "Oh, do it more," "longer," or "harder!" Most clients appear to be able to take a great deal of pressure because it has such a positive effect on them. This is particularly true in working with bones, joints, and connective tissue.

Discerning Healing Needs

Please note that, as you read, you will want to practice Healing Hover Touch to become an effective therapist. With practice and development of your own Healing Hover Touch skills, you will be able to assist others with healing needs. Sometimes, you may detect needs for healing that your practice partners will not be aware of.

However, this is not a parlor game. So when you choose a partner, remember that it is all right, if you are in pain as the client, to describe where you are in pain. And ask what the presenting complaint is if you are the practitioner. Neither partner needs to wait to see if the other can find it. Possibly you both will, eventually, with practice and experience, quickly feel the other's discomfort. In the beginning stages, feel free to discuss those pains with each other.

Learning from the Experiences of Others

Practitioners of a variety of treatment methods can discuss and learn from and support each other, and they often do so on a regular basis. The letter that follows, with a brief excerpt from another of her letters, is from a woman who now practices at least two modalities of integrative treatment; she attended a Healing Hover Touch interactive learning experience a few years ago.

There are several reasons for choosing the following two letters.

- Donna McMillan already practices a different healing modality to which she is loyal, and she continues to practice both. Using integrative treatment systems, after all, is much of what this book promotes.

- She is an American who lives in Japan, and she is closely connected to many other nationalities; she enjoys the diversity of their cultural ways, which is an advantage to her in her healing work.

- She shared both successes and what appear to have been non-successes and asked questions about them, which will allow me to share another's real-life experiences after her letter.

- She shares several other experiences, which, although there were no questions, provides me another opportunity to elaborate and to offer further information.

- Donna is one of many who teaches and encourages others in developing their Healing Hover Touch skills.

I am grateful to Donna for sharing her experiences, observations, and questions. She has given me specific permission to quote any of several letters. I will quote extensively from one letter that relates several examples of the use of Healing Hover Touch, and I will change the names of the other people in the letter. I will also quote briefly from another of Donna's letters. Numbers in parentheses—e.g., (1)—correspond to my responses, which follow the text of the letters.

Donna McMillan's letter has been edited to reveal her critical points for writing:

Dear Dr. Mosley,

Thank you for your wonderful Healing Hover Touch and your presentation of it at the conference in July in Arizona.

My friend Rosalynne from San Antonio attended your session with me, and we practiced your method there and each day of the conference thereafter, and were most impressed with the method. Rosalynne is seventy-nine and your method works splendidly for her. She is in unbelievably good shape for someone seventy-nine, but she'd been feeling a weakness behind her knees, and that was one condition we worked on. It felt as though it was the size of an egg behind each knee and in one treatment, it was gone. Rosalynne's treatments for me were equally effective.

Since my return to Tokyo, I have demonstrated your method at a sharing meeting of the practitioners of the other healing modality I am associated with. First I used it for a woman from France who was about to move to London for eight months; she had a severe pain in her neck, probably due to stress and tension. Hover Touch significantly reduced, but did not completely get rid of the pain, so I repeated it for her later.

The second time the pain went from the size of a small egg to the size of a coin a bit smaller than a U.S. quarter, though it did not completely disappear. (I don't know whether I was doing something incorrectly or insufficiently or whether certain types of conditions require repeated treatments.) (1)

However, another woman—Maria from Acapulco, Mexico—had a bad headache that two other healing modalities had not gotten rid of. It disappeared completely and did not return after Hover Touch.

I used Healing Hover Touch for James from England, who had hurt his right hand so badly in Karate (at which he is proficient) that he couldn't close it completely. He had already had treatments using two other modalities. His hand still hurt and he still couldn't completely close it. I did the Healing Hover Touch treatment on our way to the train station.

I've noticed that I begin swaying on my feet almost as soon as I begin, and the person receiving the treatment often sways, too. (2) The pain in James' right hand went from the size of a soccer ball to a grapefruit, and then it hurt somewhere else, but afterward his hand felt *much* better and he could close his hand—to his surprise!

This was the first time, however, that I'd ever gotten a negative reply to, "Are you willing to let the pain and the condition go?"

He said, "No," and I could hardly believe it. In fact I wasn't sure I had heard right and so repeated the question in different words: "Is there any bene-fit to you in keeping the pain?"

And he said, "No."

So I repeated, "Are you willing to let the pain go?"

And he said, "Well, yes and no.'"

Taken aback, I groped for words a bit and asked, "If you had to choose, would you choose to let the pain go?" and he said, "Yes," so I was able to finish the procedure.

He said afterward that he had not realized that he wasn't willing to let the pain go. It was for him a macho thing. He said, "I was injured in a Karate competition."(3)

I then treated Maria. She asked if this could be done for an emotional pain as well."(4)

Briefly, notes from another of Donna's letters are as follows:

I also appreciate the additional material about doing Hover Touch for oneself. (5) There are seven in my other health practitioner's group who also know Healing Hover Touch. Two of them had feedback to pass on to you.

The first was Maria from Acapulco, who asked me to tell you hello and to tell you she's had nearly one hundred percent results from it. The one exception is her sister's boyfriend. The summary of his situation is that he contracted a painful, but usually not fatal, disease at the same time he began a business, which quickly became successful. He believes that if he were healed, the success in his business would also disappear. (6)

The other was James—the man from England with the Karate injury—who used Hover Touch remotely over the phone with his girlfriend, visualizing each action and asking her the questions. She said she didn't feel anything, but at the end, her pain was completely gone! (7)

The following are responses to the observations or questions denoted by numbers in the text.

1. Donna expressed some concern that perhaps she had not done all that she could do to clear up her client's pain. In Chapter 4, "Instructions for Balancing Body Energy in Healing Hover Touch," the first of the basic four steps is heart centeri ng. Note that this step is considered to be the most important because it speaks to the inner life and to the intention of the practitioner. I often say to myself, "I love you" directed toward the client; "I wish you health and all good in life." With this set in mind and heart, it would be very difficult to do anything wrong. And yes, some conditions do require more than one treatment. As with any modality of treatment, some conditions may require many.

   One example was a girl whom I shall call Brittany; she was

twelve years old the first time I saw her. She had scoliosis, and even though she was in a hard body brace, her spine was severely curved. The plan was that she would wear increasingly sturdy braces and that at age eighteen she would have surgery.

Brittany's father accompanied her; they lived a considerable distance from me. I taught Mr. Smith how to treat Brittany, and he was to teach his wife. The intention was that I would see her once a year. When they departed, Brittany hugged me. The full brace felt cold, but her brilliant face was warm. In fact, the hugging became a ritual. She asked for a hug each time that we parted company.

The next year when I saw her, Brittany's back was about the same as the first time I saw her. A year later when I saw her (at the end of the second year), the curvature was more visibly pronounced even though she wore a stronger brace. I gave her one treatment each time I saw her, and the parents were to perform the treatments at least once a day in between. In talking with Brittany and her father, I discovered that the parents had divorced during the past year; her mother had moved a long distance away, and her father was traveling three to four days a week. I encouraged them to get a friend—preferably someone who truly loved Brittany, but someone at least—to give her treatments while her father was traveling.

The solution was a school friend, and the friend's mother committed to giving the treatments during the father's absence. Brittany's mother would do them when she visited. By the end of the third year, there was no visible change at all. At the end of the fourth year, there was noticeable improvement. On her seventeenth birthday, Brittany drove her father the several hundred miles to visit me. They walked into my office, and she was as straight as a rod. She immediately walked over to me and asked for a hug. No brace. No surgery in the past year and none planned. We all three cried together, and I took the two of them to dinner to celebrate.

Yes, she had at least one treatment every day for the previous three of the five years since we first met.

2. Personally, I do not sway at all unless I close my eyes, which I sometimes do when I first place my hands in front of the client's face. Actually, I think of it more as a minor weaving, and it's very brief because I do not leave my eyes closed for very long. Sometimes, the client's eyes are closed for a considerable time, but generally if he weaves at all, it is very minor. Early on, I usually say that if they begin to weave, I will touch them on the shoulder as a gentle reminder. They don't usually require any more of a reminder than that. I have never needed to do a grounding exercise for myself, but if a practitioner of any modality of which I am aware feels the need, the following works really well: Just imagine a hook being attached to your abdomen (non-painfully) just one inch below the navel and that the hook is attached to a cable that is attached to a sixty-thousand-pound stabilizing block in the middle of the earth. All weaving ceases.

3. This is a really good example of having a payoff for keeping the pain. It's good that James was able to see it. As a Karate athlete, he would in the normal course of time receive considerable attention for being a Western citizen doing as well as he did in an Eastern athletic endeavor, especially while he was injured.

   Another excellent example of a client saying "No" to releasing an illness because of a payoff is a woman we shall call Kathryn who had had cancer low in her spine for seven years. Her daughter drove her over one hundred miles to come see me on a Tuesday. The daughter, Caitlyn, was going to watch so she could do the treatments daily for Kathryn between her intended biweekly visits to me. We talked briefly before we began the treatment. Then I asked Kathryn to stand if she felt up to it, and she did. Just a few minutes into the treatment, I asked Kathryn if she was ready to give up the cancer.

   Kathryn immediately began crying and said, "No." I had heard that answer before, but Caitlyn couldn't believe her mother would say that. We sat back down and talked awhile longer. They departed a few minutes later.

On Friday, I received a call from Kathryn saying she would like to try again. We set an appointment for the following Tuesday. On Tuesday, she arrived with her husband.

We began talking about the days since we had seen each other, and I asked her "What caused the change of mind?"

Her husband said, "I can tell you that. I have been a workaholic throughout our forty years of marriage. We own a large seed and feed store in a major agricultural area a hundred miles from here and three smaller seed and feed stores in neighboring areas.

"When she came home and told me that she had said she didn't want to release her spinal cancer because she had no reason to live [which she had not said to me], I asked her, 'Why?'

"She told me that since we didn't have a life together, she didn't want to live. Then I began to cry and asked her what I could do to help us create a life together. She asked me if I would retire. We have two sons who can run all four businesses. They have always worked with me, but I still worked sixty to eighty hours a week.

"I agreed to partially retire. I've already made arrangements with our boys to run the businesses, but I don't think I'd live very long if I went from an eighty-hour workweek to nothing. So I told her I would work twenty-five to thirty hours a week and would take three- and four-day weekends off. She agreed with that and asked me to come learn how to give her the Hover Touch treatments."

I never saw them again, but in less than four months, Kathryn called and said that her cancer was beginning to reverse. Three ingredients were of primary importance to this healing: belief that she could be healed, desire to be healed, and making a decision to take action to assist the healing. A year later, Caitlyn called and said that her parents were spending three months in Arizona and planned to do so every winter. Her mother's cancer was in complete remission.

4. The answer is, yes, the method works for at least some mental-emotional problems. Note especially the boxed information entitled "Some Frequently Asked Questions (FAQs) about Healing Hover Touch," at the end of Chapter 4, "Instructions for Balancing Body Energy in Healing Hover Touch." The very first situation in which I used the Healing Hover Touch ability consciously was on behalf of a very emotionally distressed person.

5. It is possible to treat oneself if one has upper-body mobility. Because we rely on energy radiating from the hands, we can reach parts of our backs, for example, that we cannot actually touch. We know that people in Asia have used Qigong for at least four thousand years[15] and that much of their treatment has been for themselves. What is less well known is that a similar practice has been used in Alaska for at least centuries, if not millennia, as well.

   When I taught Healing Hover Touch in Alaska, I met an Eskimo woman who quickly became one of my teachers. She was in her late seventies, and, as a four-year-old, she and her ten-year-old sister had watched a moose attack their mother; when their father went to help, both parents were killed by the moose.

   The ten-year-old took care of the four-year-old, and she taught the little one everything their parents had taught her. As far as medical treatment went, there were no hospitals, pharmacies, or practitioners of any kind nearby. They used self-treatment. What she described could well be Qigong, Healing Hover Touch, Therapeutic Touch, or Healing Touch. About the only thing she added each time was that she rubbed her hands together for every treatment, so that the friction would get her hands extra warm. Generally, I only do that occasionally for treatment of my own or others' eyes. She pointed out that she needed the extra warmth.

6. If a person carried such a belief (i.e., that if he was healed, a successful business venture would disappear along with the

healing of the disease), it is reasonable that such a person would be hesitant to submit to treatment of *any* kind. Even if the person could be cajoled into trying the treatment, it is also reasonable to believe that the chances of success would be considerably diminished. The point has been made previously that unbelief does not necessarily prevent a healing. Even submitting to a treatment while one is resisting often does not prevent the healing. But belief does help, and, failing that, a *desire* for a healing is very helpful.

An example of the effect of the three ingredients mentioned above working together on the part of the client(s) is from a learning experience I facilitated in Santurce, Puerto Rico. A friend, Carmen Venus Baerga, was the translator. However, I still know enough Spanish to get into trouble. Instead of speaking the request for a volunteer demonstration model in English and allowing Carmen Venus to translate, I asked for one volunteer in Spanish myself. The result was that seven people came forward and onto the platform.

I decided to proceed by working with all seven, one at a time. When I was finished with the first, the other six all laughed and said they were also healed; they went back to their seats, which prompted laughter in the other four hundred participants.

The three ingredients all seven people who were healed demonstrated, once again, were belief, desire, and willingness to participate fully. The six had stood to one side, but did everything I had asked the model to do. Those factors raise the likelihood of success.

7. Remember James, who used Healing Hover Touch remotely over the phone to his girlfriend, visualizing each action and asking her the questions? She didn't feel anything while he was doing that, but at the conclusion of the distant treatment, her pain was completely gone. James had used "nonlocal mind," to use Dossey's term. In other words, this is one facet of Era III medicine. "*Nonlocal* does not mean merely 'a long way off' or a 'very long time' but, rather *infinitude* in space

and time. If something is nonlocal it is *unlimited*."[15]

I've had numerous such experiences through the years. Sometimes I use Healing Hover Touch remotely, and sometimes I simply pray with clients and get the same or similar results. Much of what I do is related to what the client has asked for. For those of Christian belief, you will recall that Jesus did what seemed to be called for in relation to the specific individual. For some, he simply pronounced the word that they were healed. For the centurion's servant, he pronounced the word in absentia. For the blind man, he placed a spittle of mud on his eyes and told him to go bathe in the River Jordan seven times. For those whose beliefs are inspired by Buddha, Abraham, and luminaries of the other six of the world's nine great religions (Islam, Hinduism, Taoism, Confucianism, Zoroastrianism, and global Native Spirituality), examples are legion.

So, too, for medical practitioners. Practitioners do what seems to be needed: Given similar symptoms, using Era I methods, for one patient they may give an aspirin, for a second a placebo, for a third propoxyphene hydrochloride (Darvon), and for a fourth meperidine (Demerol). Or, as in the case below, a physician used Era III method and simply "thought" about the patient.

My first experience of a physician using distance treatment—or nonlocal mind—was vicarious. In 1969, I hosted a tour to the Soviet Union. When we were touring in the "outback" from Moscow, one of our group fell and was hurt fairly seriously. Two people had to help her walk, and even then she was in great pain. She was unable to get off the tour bus to do any sightseeing the rest of the day.

We attempted to get medical assistance, but none was available nearby. Since we could not find a doctor locally, our Intourist guide called an M.D. in Moscow. I talked to him first, and then the injured tour member talked with him. He told her to sit quietly while he "*thought* about her healing." Notice he did not say he was going to pray for her. They sat silently for twenty minutes before he spoke again. He suggested that she stop to see him when we returned to Moscow. She improved considerably during that twenty minutes of silence. She was able to walk without help, although she limped slightly. By the next day, she did not limp and did not miss any of the considerable walking we were scheduled to do. She did not need to see the doctor when we returned to Moscow.

Shortly after returning to the United States, I read a news magazine article that described in detail how Russian doctors practiced distance treatments. They did not believe in prayer, but they believed in two extra senses, intuition and mental telepathy. They used both of these in their distance treatments. There were—and my visit to Russia in 1993 confirmed that there still are—great expanses of areas (there are eleven time zones across Russia, with no consideration for the other former Soviet Socialist Republics) with few people and virtually no medical facilities or practitioners, so physicians were taught to use distance healing techniques.

One experience of my own in recent years along these lines was quite spontaneous. I was leaving my home on a weekend business trip. I had packed, said goodbye to my wife, and had already taken my luggage to my car in the garage. Then I realized I had forgotten something in our bedroom upstairs. I went back, took the item out of my desk, and suddenly I thought, "My brother Jim, I don't know where you are or what's happening, but I want you to know that I love you and I'm praying for you." When I passed by my wife downstairs again, she asked me what I had said. It was then that I realized I did not just *think* that thought, but that I had *said it so loudly* in the bedroom that Martha thought I was talking to her downstairs. I told her, "No, I was talking to Jim."

She just said, "Oh." One might have guessed that I did that sort of thing often, but I didn't and I don't. On the other hand, it has happened on other occasions and with a variety of relationships. I prayed for Jim all the way to the airport as I drove, and periodically the rest of that day and the next day.

When Martha tracked me down the next day after hearing from our sister-in-law, Lois, it was to tell me that Jim had had a heart attack at the very time that I had said what I did to him; he was eight hundred miles away. It is also noteworthy that, although Jim was having the heart attack when I "spoke" to him, he did not yet know that the distress he was experiencing was, in fact, a heart attack. I'm happy to say that he recovered nicely.

———(o)———

Now, we turn to the question, "How does one do Healing Hover Touch?" The next chapter outlines specific instructions and techniques as a place to start. Notice there are very few rules to follow unwaveringly, but there are suggestions for the early stages in developing your Healing Hover Touch skills.

Instructions for Balancing Body Energy in Healing Hover Touch

A practitioner is the external facilitator of healing energy, or Qi. Qi is much of what you will bring to your clients' healing needs. What follows are techniques that will help you as you begin. These techniques will initially help you in helping the client balance their energy. You may come back to the techniques repeatedly, but the techniques are not the important factor. What *is* important is that, through balancing body energy, you help the client regain and sustain her state of health and wholeness. It is also important that you show up and are able to help—able to present yourself as a vessel through which good things can happen.

Do you remember how stiffly you performed when you first learned to drive? You may have learned to drive so long ago that you do not remember all the details, but you may remember that you felt awkward about it. But that awkward and laborious insert-key-in-ignition, put-left-foot-on-clutch, put-right-foot-on-gas pedal, put-in-gear stage is gone now. Even those who learned to drive a car without a clutch felt awkward.

That happens with healing techniques, too. They help you at

first, but after a while you forget the technique because you begin using healing skills as an extension of your life experience. There is nothing dogmatic about the techniques, but the inner life of the practitioner and her intentions for the good of the recipient are of the utmost importance.

Now, having made this point, let me list the basic four steps that I have developed for practicing Healing Hover Touch; they serve as guides for the techniques that follow.

- Heart centering
- Assessment
- Balancing energy, including clearing and upgrading
- Closure

The above basic four steps will always be with you, and you will want to review and use them most of the time, depending on the situation you are invited into, as guides for your energy balancing treatments.

Heart Centering. This step is the most important step for me; it is virtually tethered to my bones. The inner life, or prayer life, of a practitioner is important to coming to a healing task as a clear vessel of love and goodwill. That inner life is necessary for being attuned to the client, wholly present, and fully focused. As is noted elsewhere in this book, it is important that the practitioner's intention be to visualize the highest and best good for the client, so that the healer is able to serve as a facilitator of healing energy and not be attached to the outcome—which generally creates practitioner anxiety. We neither credit nor blame ourselves for the outcome.

Assessment. By passing our hands over the person, front and back and from head to toe, we may discover needs the client was unaware of when he asked for assistance.

Balancing Energy. This activity looks much like the assessment, but it has a different intention. The second time through, you are not necessarily looking for (or, more accurately, feeling for) changes in body temperatures, although you may sense something that you did not catch during the assessment step. What you will be doing is "clearing up" negative body energies, which may show up as hot or cold spots, or which you may sense as a general malaise. On the positive side, you will be upgrading (from Step 5c below): "The practitioner looks for wellness in the client's body that can be used to assist in balancing the client's body energy. The practitioner may also visualize for the client health not actually being experienced at the moment."

Closure. This basic step looks similar to Step 6 (below), and it is identical to Step 22. "While standing in front of the client, with the fingers of both your hands touching each other, pass your hands over the crown chakra down to the shoulders (back of neck) behind the head, and then bring the hands back over the top of the head (since it is probable that during the treatment you have opened the crown chakra). Then continue down in front of the face again as a way of 'sealing,' so that positive energy is not lost through the crown chakra."

There are no hard and fast rules saying that the above sequence must not be varied. On the contrary, the basic steps may be completed out of sequence; or, depending on time and circumstances, one or more steps may be eliminated entirely.

For example, in an emergency, you may not need to do an assessment, because the immediate need is likely to be clear. You may repeat one or more of the above four steps several times while omitting one or two altogether.

The following twenty-two steps are refinements to accomplish the basic four steps above.

Heart Centering (Steps 1–3)

1. When you are practicing Healing Hover Touch, decide which partner is to be the practitioner first and which is going to be the client. For this practice session, assume the person does not have a headache or a specific pain, but he doesn't feel

very well in general. You are looking to rebalance the energy. The client has no presenting complaint beyond the fact of not feeling very well. (If the client is ambulatory, he should stand so you can walk all the way around him.)

2. It is assumed that you come to this moment of working with another's body energy in a state of prayer. Even with that being so, you will take more time for heart centering mentally, emotionally, and through prayer or meditative silence before you begin.

3. It is important to remind yourself that you are an instrument, ready and willing, and that you are a facilitator of healing energy. Visualize that the very highest good may be manifest in the client's life and affairs. Specifically, you are there to assist the client's health—physical, mental, emotional, and spiritual. (This is why Step 2 above is so vital.) I often feel that the greatest gift I bring to a client is a statement I may say to myself, and feel and send to the client: "I love you."

Assessment (Steps 4–6)

4. You may determine how you may be of greatest service by any or all of the following approaches, not necessarily in this order:

- A total balancing of the client's body energy
- Observation of the client's body, position, or facial expressions
- Using your intuition
- Asking the client where the problem is or what he wishes you to do for him. Usually, I ask about presenting complaints last; I have often discovered conditions the client was unaware of, and I have questioned whether I would have made the discovery if my attention had been distracted first by an identified presenting complaint.

An example of one experience I had when I was not distracted by knowing a presenting complaint was when a young woman I will call Mary Ann, who had cancer, told me that she had a tumor on her left side. She had had both chemotherapy and radiation, and the tumor was reducing in size. She told me that she had received an MRI the day before and that that tumor was all that still showed.

During the assessment, I felt what I believed to be a tumor on the lower right side. As I passed my left hand over the area of the lower right abdomen, it felt to me as though a gurgling sound was suddenly choked off. I did not *hear* gurgling, I only felt it; keep in mind I did not actually come in contact with her body. When I completed the assessment, I asked Mary Ann about the possibility of a tumor on the right side, and she repeated, "I do not have one there; I just had an MRI yesterday." Her mother was with her in my office, and I told them both about the gurgling feeling I had sensed. I encouraged Mary Ann to go see her doctor as soon as possible. She protested, but her mother (who had attended a workshop and had seen healings happen throughout the evening just a few days previously) assured me that they would go to the doctor. The mother, who is a veterinarian, told me she had been a total skeptic until she attended that workshop.

A few days later, the mother left a message with an assistant saying that Mary Ann had had emergency surgery that next morning and that the surgeon had removed three-quarters of a gallon of tumor. The surgeon also said that patients usually need transfusions because operating on tumors such as hers normally creates considerable blood loss. He said that this was a strange tumor; it was as though the blood supply had been totally cut off.

It is all right to ask about complaints or problems—and I do, but usually after I set my intention of good and do my assessment of perceived needs.

5. Begin by setting an intention of good for the client, along with an assessment and a general balancing of the client's body energy. If the practitioner were a physician, this might be called a diagnosis.

When she is making an assessment, the practitioner attempts three tasks simultaneously:

- The practitioner looks for physical limitations of which the client may not be aware.
- The practitioner uses energy in an effort to assist the client by both "clearing" of negative body energy, which may show up as hot or cold spots, and by upgrading (see the next item).
- The practitioner looks for wellness in the client's body that can be used to assist in balancing the client's body energy. The practitioner may also visualize for the client health not actually being experienced at the moment.

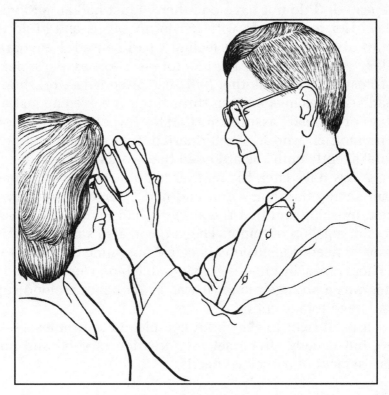

Step 5

(The practitioner accomplishes the foregoing assessment and balancing tasks of item 5 by continuing through item 22.)

Continue by placing your hands in front of the client's face (take a few seconds to a couple of minutes if you need to). You are looking for the client's ambient level of energy, heat, or warmth (easily detected through indoor clothing or casts)—whatever that feels like to you—so that you know what the rest of the body should feel like. Areas of the body where the energy is not in balance may feel unusually warm, hot, cool, cold, congested, or tingling. If there is an infection in the head or face, it will likely feel so different from your own hands (often noticeably warm or even hot) that you will not have to ask if there is an infection in the head or face.

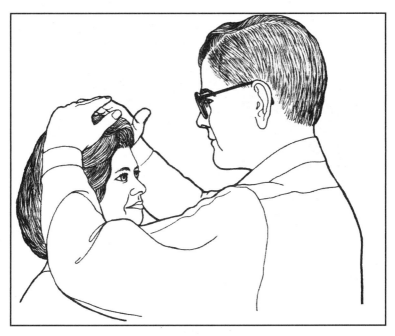

Step 6

6. With the fingers of both hands touching each other, pass your hands, palms down, over the top of the head. What you are feeling for is the crown chakra (same area as the soft spot on the head of an infant). Is there any coolness (or heat) up

there? Is that something you feel the need to attend to later? (If you feel any change in temperature along the way, that is a point you will want to come back to later. Do not stop now. Finish balancing out the energy.)

Balancing Energy (Steps 7–21)

7. Move your hands down to the shoulders behind the neck, and then pass them back over the top of the head, moving your hands back to the front of the face. When you do that, bring your hands down and let your thumbs touch one another under the chin.

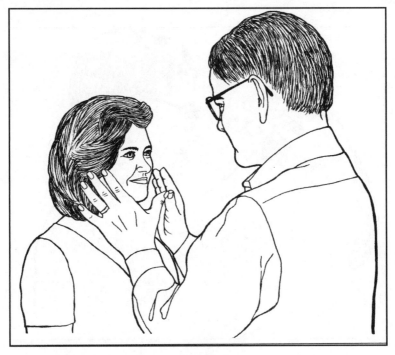

Step 7

8. Separate your hands so you can go out over the shoulders and down over the outer meridians of the arms to the hands.

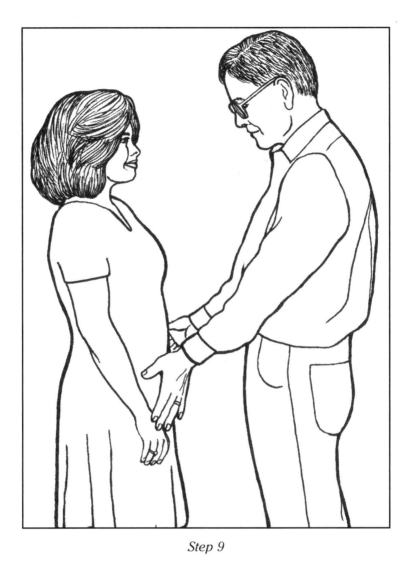

Step 9

9. Move your hands all the way down the arms and then bring your hands back up the *front* of the client's arms.

10. When you get back to the head and shoulder area, rejoin your thumbs under the client's chin.

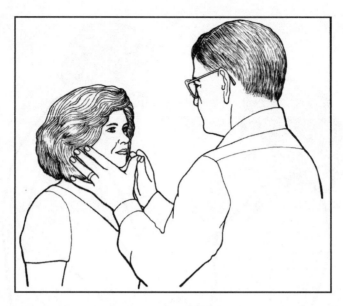

Step 10

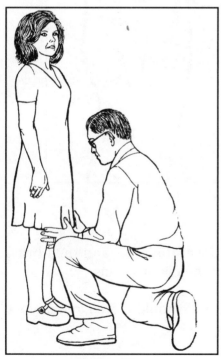

Step 11

11. Move your hands down in front of the client (over the chest, abdomen, and legs) kneeling in front of the client, all the way down to the toes. (You can feel through shoes, boots, or even body casts, as well as normal indoor clothing.)

12. Move your hands back up from the toes, all the way up the front to just in front of the throat. (The inner and outer meridians you are following by going over the breastbone down to the toes and over the arms to the hands are the same

meridians—the series of complicated channels that network the body—that both Eastern and Western acupuncturists and acupressurists use.)

13. With your thumbs still together, move your hands up under the throat, and then walk around the side of the person with your hands as close to the neck as you can keep them until you are behind the person. Your thumbs should still be together with your hands right behind the client's neck.

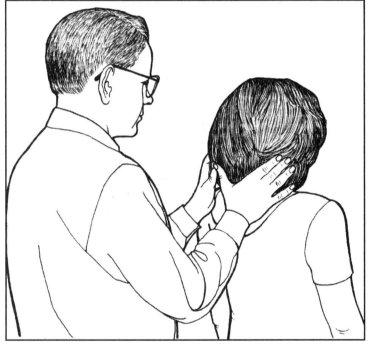

Step 13

14. Repeat Step 6 from behind the client.

15. Move your hands down over the shoulders and the outside edges of the arms. Typically, your hands should be some-where between an inch and three inches away from the body. Even though you may feel energy at a greater distance, the

client will feel your energies more effectively if your hands are approximately two inches away.

16. Once you have moved your hands down the sides of the arms, move up along the backs of the arms.

17. Bring your hands back together behind the neck, thumbs together again.

18. Start out by moving your hands down the back, over the shoulder blades as you did when you were in front of the client. Your thumbs may have to separate as you get closer to the floor, but keep them together as long as possible [allows you closest contact with the greatest number of channels, or meridians].

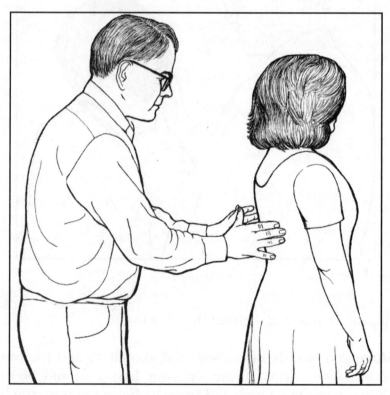

Step 18

19. Move all the way down to the floor behind the heels. (If a person is lying in a hospital bed, sitting in furniture, or sitting in a wheelchair, move your hands over whatever part of the body you have access to.)

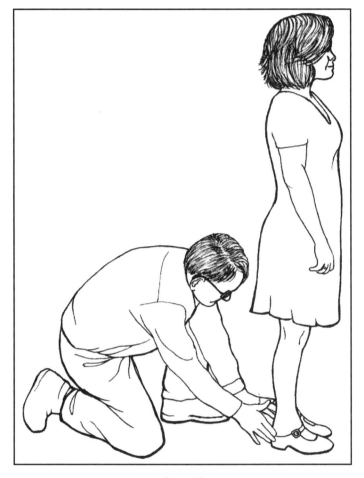

Step 19

20. Move your hands back up to the back of the client's neck.

21. Put your thumbs together again, and move back around to the front (on the opposite side of the client from where you were

before), keeping your hands near the neck as you move back in front again.

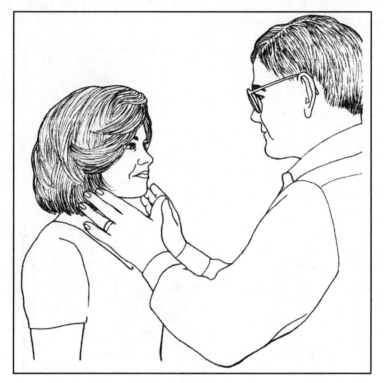

Step 21

Review of Balancing Procedures

If the client has a presenting complaint or you have found a need of which the client is unaware, this is when you would put the ends of your index and middle fingers just above the person's eyes, always asking for permission first. It may startle the client if her eyes are closed and you place your fingers above the eyes on the forehead without asking for permission.

Whether or not you have discovered a need the client has during the assessment time, ask if there is a presenting complaint, pain, condition, or discomfort. It does not have to be a raging pain. It can just be a simple discomfort or a known condition with no pain. I want to restate for emphasis: with anything that is painful or uncomfortable, or a condition anywhere in the body, *initially* we work with the face and forehead, with the fingertips on the forehead above the eyes, even though the pain, discomfort, or condition may be elsewhere in the body. We may or may not need to attend to the actual site later.

At some point about now, ask the client, "Are you ready to give up the pain?" (or discomfort or condition—use as specific a name as is known to you). If a client rushes too quickly to an "Of course!" type of answer, I ask the question again and ask them to be thoughtful about the response. In fact, I usually ask it two or three ways, just in case they don't recognize themselves in the first question.

For example, a second way to ask might be a simple, "Are you sure you want to release the condition (by a specific name, when it is known)?" A variation might be, "Are you sure there is no pay-off for keeping the condition?"

Sometimes, a client may have controlled others by using the condition—unwittingly or perhaps even consciously. Being help-less, fragile, etc., gives some people previously unknown power.

I have asked these questions in classes in working with volunteer demonstration models, and people have begun crying and finally have said, "No." I've also had clients who came for treatment to my office and have not proceeded when I asked these questions.

Once the willingness to release the condition has been established, the practitioner may say something like, "Now, I'm going to put my hands in front of your face briefly, and what I'm going to be looking for is a heat or energy level. Close your eyes, take a deep breath, and hold. Breathe out just as deeply. Again, breathe in very deeply, hold, and breathe out just as deeply. And again, breathe in very deeply, hold, and breathe out just as deeply. Resume breathing normally, and continue to relax." This breathing exercise is part of internal Qigong, which is what the client is doing for herself.

Then, ask what color the pain or discomfort is, what size it is, and where it is located. Ask the color, size, and location questions a second and a third time if necessary. The pain does not actual-ly shift from one place to another. Rather, once the primary pain is gone, the secondary pain becomes noticeable and the pain only appears to shift locations. When the secondary pain is gone, the tertiary pain becomes the primary, and usually, the third is the last level of pain. If the pain lasts through three questions of color, size, and location, and a vestige remains, that is when I draw the pain and the cause of the pain together to cause it to rise and exit through the crown chakra.

Often, the questions are all that is needed to eliminate pain. Continue, however, until you have also dealt with the cause of the pain. At that point, direct the pain and the cause of the pain to rise up and go out through the crown chakra on the count of three. You may want to say something similar to the following: "We draw the pain and the cause of that pain together like a ball of congealed energy. That ball of congealed energy reduces in size until it is the size of a small green pea, soft as cotton candy that would dissolve in the rain. The pain and the cause of the pain rise up and go out through the crown chakra on the count of three. Going up . . . one. Going up . . . two. Going up . . . three, and it is gone." (I usually snap my fingers on the count of "three.")

If the client tells you where there is a discomfort that you may or may not have identified when you were doing the general energy assessment and balancing, you can go back to that area and work on it specifically. (Congestion in the face and head may feel inordi-nately warm or even hot, or, occasionally, cool; conversely, infec-tion in the body may feel cool or even cold, or, occasionally, warm.)

Once you have again located the imbalanced energy or an area that the client has told you is uncomfortable or painful, move your hand in either a clockwise or counterclockwise motion over the area. (Do it both ways; it does not matter which is first.) Then move your hand over the area up and down in a straight line, and from side to side.

When you care enough to share external Qigong, healthy clients may feel relaxed, and they will often report feeling as though they had just had a twenty-minute nap. Caring is not the level of discomfort you have for others' suffering. Accept their experience as their experience. Change conditions where possible; assume neither credit nor guilt for others' experiences. As practitioners, we cannot control the outcome.

Closure (Step 22)

22. While you are standing in front of the client, with the fingers of both your hands touching each other, pass your hands over the crown chakra down to the shoulders (back of the neck) behind the head, and then bring the hands back over the top of the head (since during the treatment you probably have opened the crown chakra). Then continue down in front of the face again as a way of sealing, so that positive energy is not lost through the crown chakra.

If you are practicing this exercise with another person, you may now wish to switch roles as practitioner and client.

Some Frequently Asked Questions (FAQs) About Healing Hover Touch

How did you begin the practice that you have named Healing Hover Touch?

In 1962, I was a young minister in a church on the East Coast of the United States. I did a great deal of prayer counseling as well as psychological counseling. One day, I received a request for a counseling appointment from Esther, a woman who told me she had just "fired" her Manhattan psychiatrist, whom she had seen three times a week for seventeen years. A friend had suggested she come to see me. Actually, this friend had never seen me herself; she had called me, and I listened to her and prayed with her. She had told Esther that she was healed before she hung up the phone.

While the referral by Esther's friend was reassuring, the idea that I was to replace a psychiatrist of seventeen years' standing most assuredly was not!

Esther came to see me for her Friday appointment in a chauffeur-driven limousine. As we met, it took all my training and experience as a non-anxious presence to keep me from reacting visibly to what I was seeing.

We went into my office and were seated. For single-person counseling, I had two comfortable chairs facing each other in front of my desk so there would be no desk or other furniture between us. Esther appeared to be a pale and exhausted, approximately seventy-three-year-old woman; her legs, arms, and head flailed uncontrollably. The flailing was not constant, but frequent, with movement that approximated a puppet being controlled by a puppeteer.

I had seen many people with physical disabilities who had erratic movements, but Esther's movements appeared to derive from the psyche. Part of that assessment was based on what I had learned from her when we made the appointment. Basically, I felt that few people who were seeing her for the first time would think of the behavior as a result of physical incapacity.

Esther began telling me her story. Quite honestly, I could hardly hear her for the distraction of seeing her bodily movements. I had a background in psychology, and I had completed a hospital psychiatric internship for clergy, but I had never seen this behavior, nor did I have a name for what I was seeing.

Although I wasn't as comfortable in psychological counseling as I was in prayer counseling, it seemed apparent to me that I was going to have to give psychological counseling a try at least. *Perhaps,* I thought, *after a session or two I can refer her to a different psychiatrist.* During the first twenty-plus minutes that she talked, my mind was racing through all of my feelings of insecurity about my ever being able to help her. I said to myself several times, "You're just not equipped to help this woman." All the while, Esther's legs, arms, and head bobbed, quite uncontrollably, but almost always only one at a time.

Periodically, when one of her limbs or her head bobbed, she would ask, "There, did you see that? They're controlling me. Do you see those strings?"

I asked, "Who is controlling you?"

She answered, "*They* are." This happened several times in the first fifteen to twenty minutes.

As the time neared thirty minutes and I had said very little to Esther, except to ask who controlled her (although I had said much to myself), I finally stood up and interrupted her.

As I moved toward her chair slowly, I said, "I'd like you to stop talking now, and I'd like us to pray together. But I want you to keep your eyes open and watch what I'm going to do." I showed her my right hand as I was making a scissors-like motion with it. "I'm going to cut all those strings 'they' are controlling you with." By this time I had been standing in front of her for several seconds and her flailing feet had each kicked me once. Her head and arms were also still flailing.

I was wondering what my colleagues in either religion or psychology would think if they knew what I was about to do and what I had already said. I was determined that they would never hear about it from me!

As I began to snip the several strings "attached" to her head, without touching the top of her head, I said, "See, I'm cutting these strings so 'they' can no longer control you." Much to my amazement, her head immediately stopped bobbing about. (I don't think I said it out loud, but I'm pretty sure I said to myself, "Holy cow!"—a natural reference, since I grew up to age twelve on a farm.)

I continued "cutting" strings, first down over one shoulder, arm, and hand, and then the other, again never actually touching her. Both arms immediately relaxed and were peaceful. So far, so good. Just as I leaned down to pass over her legs, she kicked me one more time. However, to my knowledge and belief, that was the last time any part of her body flailed out of control.

However, I did not step back immediately to "admire" my work. Instead, I had a concern. In 1962, television sets had vacuum tubes in them. When a tube was weak, reception would become fuzzy or static would be created. Lacking remote controls then, the viewer would go to the set to adjust the picture and it would clear up, sometimes without the viewer ever touching the set. The person would step back from the set, and immediately the screen would again be fuzzy or have a snow blizzard or there were walking "phantoms." Even if one had made adjustments, these blurred phenomena still often occurred when the viewer moved away from the set. Even the least sophisticated in the field of electronics knew that the human body's energy was somehow assisting the electronics of the set.

I wondered whether my presence in front of Esther was reassuring enough to her that the alteration in her behavior would change when I stepped away from her. On the other hand, it was clear that neither of us would be able to spend the rest of our lives in that office. So I returned to my chair, backing up all the way because I wanted to see what might happen, and I sat down. We talked awhile longer, closed with prayer, and she left my office.

On Sunday morning, a new couple was attending services. In a small church, it's always easy to notice first-timers. I guessed that the woman was in her early forties and the man was in his late fifties.

After worship, the new man approached me with a hand extended and said, "I want to thank you for what you did for my wife."

As I took his hand, I answered, "You're welcome." Hesitatingly, I asked, "Who is your wife?"

"The woman sitting next to me in church," was his response. Naturally, I had assumed he might say that, but I was pretty sure I had never seen her before. However, as she approached us, I looked closely at her eyes and realized I *had* seen her before—on Friday, in fact. She was Esther. Esther was not seventy-three years of age (my Friday afternoon guess), nor was she forty-three (my Sunday morning guess). Both she and her husband were sixty-three.

Esther became a volunteer at the church during weekdays, served in the youth education department for a number of years, and stayed in the church until well after I had moved from there. Sam attended occasionally on Sundays after that. Esther was in the church for several hours a day, four days a week. She stayed in the church until they moved south after retirement.

This single experience caused me to reflect on occasions

when, as a teenager, I had had similar (though less dramatic) experiences with people, and even earlier experiences I had had on the farm, with both farm animals and pets. With these experiences behind me, I often used my hands in similar ways with people needing healing, but I did not speak of it outside those appointments, nor did I teach it for another seven years.

I couldn't tell if I was actually feeling coolness or the air conditioner blowing on my hands.

What you do in that case is change places in the room and see if the coolness changes. Move to a different part of the room to see if it makes any difference. Sometimes, that may be blood circulation you are dealing with. Once when I did a workshop at a healing symposium, I had a woman who said, "This feels like an air conditioner down here," as she pointed to her client's legs. I knew the woman who was the client, and I knew she had poor circulation. I said, "Move, and see if that makes any difference." I knew the heat was on in the auditorium. They moved, and the client's legs were still cold. We had a private conversation after the workshop. Fortunately, she went to see her health care provider and prevented possible complications.

How can you tell whether the warmth you feel in front of the face is from the face or from their breathing?

In that case, ask the client to breathe with their mouth closed and see if that makes any difference. Be sure you are not in front of either the mouth or the nose so that heat from the breath alone won't influence your assessment. I have done that, and I say, "Just for a moment, breathe through your nose and don't open your mouth." Then I try again.

What do you do when you feel a cool spot at the crown chakra?

I suggest you go over that spot two or three times. If you go over it and you detect that it is still cool, I would move my hand around it in a circular motion just as I would if this were the appendix or an arm. I move my hand around over the spot in a clockwise circle, then back around counterclockwise (it's not essential which direction you do first), and then just straight over it two or three times. Some of my clients have said, "I can feel the drainage." What has happened is that there is a release in the passages in the head. The clients are able to get the drainage out through the nasal and mouth passages, and then they can spit it up.

What if there is no pain, but there is something wrong?

As you practice Healing Hover Touch and you become experienced at it, you can often tell where the problem is and deal with it. It is possible to feel problems the client doesn't know of. You treat the client, and you tell them what you felt.

How Healing Hover Touch Worked for a "Spiritual Klutz"

In one Healing Hover Touch series of classes, there was an older adult couple who had three adult sons, all of whom were married. The older woman, Harriet, and the three daughters-in-law were devout in their spiritual pursuits. The sons described themselves as "semi-religious," and the father, Patrick—although he attended religious services regularly—thought of himself as an unaware "spiritual klutz." The family of eight came to the first Tuesday evening class, although Patrick protested.

After I did a preliminary demonstration with a volunteer, the students were paired off and I was walking among them. Patrick was practicing the balancing of energy over Harriet's entire body with his hands, passing over her as he knelt in front of her, and then he realized he had stopped his left hand at her lower right abdomen. He went on down, and when he came up, his left hand stopped at the same spot again. He began looking for me; I was watching him from across the room. Patrick invited me over, and he said, "I must be doing this wrong." Then he passed his hand over the spot clockwise, counterclockwise, and then up and down. Patrick asked me to check the cold spot. I did, and it was not a passive cold. It felt as if an air conditioner were blowing at me. I tried to rebalance the body energy, and the abdomen remained quite cold. I asked her if she still had her appendix, and she indicated that she did. I asked if she ever had any problem with it, and she said, "No." I told her, "I really think you should go and get it checked out." She said, "Okay, I'll make an appointment to do that." I said, "No, I mean go right now."

Harriet objected mildly, but she went to a nearby MediQuick emergency care center and they sent her to the hospital. Between five and six o'clock the next morning, the hospital removed her appendix because it was ready to rupture.

Harriet Reveals She Knew All Along

I went to see Harriet that day, but it was two or three days later before Harriet could talk coherently. I said, "I want to ask you the question I asked you Tuesday night. Have you had any problem with your appendix?"

She responded, "Don't think I haven't thought about that since I woke up from the surgery." She added, "Yes, the truth is, I knew this was coming. About six weeks ago, a little mouse nipped me in there" (pointing to her abdomen). She said, "It was a really intense, very sharp little pain, but it was a little pain, not big. It didn't last long, so I said, 'Oh, well, nothing.' Two or three days later, a little mouse nipped me again right here," as she again pointed to her abdomen. Harriet said that had happened a few times over a period of about six weeks. It had happened as many as three times in a day, and she had even said she was going to a doctor to get it checked—but she put it off. The last time she felt the mouse-like nip was the Saturday before the Tuesday night class in which her husband felt the hot appendix, which—on the outside—felt cold.

Remember that Patrick was the spiritual klutz.

Years later, Harriet had a major heart attack and was scheduled for open heart surgery. The day before the surgery I joined with Patrick, and their three adult children and their wives, and using Healing Hover Touch, we intervened again.

An Example of Healing Hover Touch at Work

I attended a lecture by Andrew Weil, M.D., in early 1998 in Kansas City, Missouri. He called anecdotes "uncontrolled observations" and said that those who insist they are "just anecdotes" do so at their own peril.

A physician and medical researcher of equally high reputation from New England said to me recently, "I know what happens to the patients [clients] when they are put in touch with you 'healers.' When I finish a couple of research projects I'm in the midst of, I would like to get about a dozen of you [healers] together and study what happens inside you as you do your work." I welcome that prospect. Such a project may well bring us one step closer to the fully recognized modalities of treatment practiced in Eastern medicine.

In 1982, a frantic mother asked me to visit her seventeen-year-old son in the hospital. He had had a motorcycle accident and was about to have his right leg amputated. Jimmie was in a body cast, and all four limbs were dangling in the air, also in casts. Many bones throughout his body were broken or fractured, but the right leg was shattered; there was nothing that could be set. The planned amputation was to be a preemptive strike against the "inevitability" of gangrene. On my first visit, I treated his entire body with either hover touch or actual touch, through the casts.

The next day, I went in and they had changed the cast because the swelling was down so much that the cast was no longer tight enough. Two or three days later, they had to change the cast on the right leg again. To make a long story short, the young man now walks with a little bit of a limp. He is about thirty-five years old now, and I last saw him at age thirty-two. He still has his leg; the bones were never set, although the bone fragments seem to have knitted together. Gangrene never developed. His leg is fairly stiff, but his leg is still there. God only knows how all of that happened.

During the night after our visit, blood was drawn and studied and in the morning the surgeon delayed surgery for a day, then two days, and three, and at the end of the week Harriet went home without surgery and with no detectable signs of muscle damage to the heart.

Practitioners who work with body energy realignment have an abundance of anecdotes that are similar. Serious illness. Dramatic and often quick recovery. At other times recovery may not be quick or dramatic, but steady and slow. Sometimes, as with all therapies, healing does not occur

Next, let's look at one more example where healing did occur.

CHAPTER SIX

The Personal Story of a Real Klutz

The following personal anecdote relates behavior I recommend to no one. My appendix ruptured, and I didn't go to a doctor for five days. If you have a ruptured appendix, I suggest you seek the services of a surgeon immediately.

My appendix ruptured while I was delivering an evening lecture in 1981. I have a very high tolerance for pain, which can be a two-edged sword. One may not suffer much pain, but one also may not get help when they need it. However, I did have enough pain that I *knew* better than to wait five days; I just did not *do* better.

As I stood behind the lectern, I raised my right leg to ease the pain, thinking no one saw me do it. I paused, took a couple of deep breaths, and went right on through the lecture as though nothing had happened. The audience was about 250 people, about half of whom I knew minimally to very well, and the other half of whom I did not know. Nobody knew there was anything wrong with me except the people who knew me really well.

My mother was present at the lecture. She was a nurse, and when I was a child, I thought she was frighteningly intuitive. She came out afterwards to where I stood in the foyer, opened my jacket, and as only a mother might do, put her hand down on my lower right side and said, "You have to go the hospital right now."

I feigned surprise and asked, "What are you talking about?"

She replied, "Your appendix just ruptured." I protested, but she said, "Don't try to kid me; I know what happened. I saw your foot raised in the air. Just look at how distended your abdomen is. You have to go." But I didn't. I hasten to add, Mother *did* know best, and I should have gone to the hospital.

The True Healing Reveals Itself

The following Monday, I arrived at the doctor's office at 8:00 in the morning. He came out to the reception room, looked at me, and said to my escort, "Take him to the hospital. I'll call the emergency room." The physician didn't even touch me; he didn't talk to me. He just looked at me and said, "Take him to the hospital."

By midnight, a surgeon who was called home from a skiing trip had tapped my appendix. The appendix was so bad by that time that he wouldn't take it out—he just drained it. When the surgeon came to see me the next morning, he said, "I want to tell you, someone with a capital *S* really loves you. That was the strangest set of circumstances I have ever seen. Normally, with a ruptured appendix that far along, the toxins would have been so pervasive throughout the whole system you'd have been dead before I could have seen you. I don't know how you made it to the hospital, except to say that the poison was wrapped as though it was in a cocoon." Two months later, the surgeon removed my appendix.

During the five days between the rupture of my appendix and the first surgery, anytime I felt pain, which was almost constantly, I repeated a Hindu mantra of sacred syllables used in affirmation and blessing (from the Sanskrit): "Om Mani Padme Hum." I have come to believe that the mantra may have enveloped the appendix and the poisons in a cocoon that slowed the spread of the poison; it saved my life until the skills of a surgeon could give further relief in the cause of healing.

If your appendix ruptures, don't seek a health food store supplement or a chiropractor. Praying or chanting a mantra is good anytime, but you should also be on your way to get the services of a surgeon.

A New View of Struggle

Just as struggling through grief over the loss of a significant other, or struggling through problems we have created, can make us much stronger, so can struggling through the "dark night" of illness make us stronger and leave us with a new view of life.

A person takes on new ways of viewing life. Have you ever really felt differently after you got well from a physical condition that you conquered? The grass is greener and the clouds aren't as heavy and the sky is a little bluer because you see life differently. You may realize that the constraints by which you have been living have been burdensome to you and you are ready to give them up. A new choice may be simply expressed, "I don't have to do that anymore." Our new outlook may be enough not only to help us feel more peaceful but also to buoy us up in the face of still other disease.

With a fresh view, the person makes new choices and creates new behaviors. The healthy new view may cause him or her to say, "No, I don't want to experience that disease again. No, I don't have to do that again. So, in order not to do that again, I am going to make some changes." The new viewpoint allows one to see the difference between a life determined by oneself and a life determined by a myriad of others.[16] We may respond to what our parents, siblings, spouse, children, our aunts and uncles, teachers, and friends thought or think we should be like. And sometimes our behavior is a response to what we think all those others think. We may try to be like all those other roles, and that decision may cause us to become sick. Once we

continued, next page

A New View of Struggle, cont.

are beyond the sickness, we may decide to be different and to make changes that allow us to live a healthier life.

The mind-body connection is a mutually reinforcing system. Renewed health brings a new round of optimism, and renewed optimism contributes to upward spirals of improved physical health. The cycles repeat themselves, and the person begins to feel more control over their life choices and therefore over some of life's experiences.

Some actions do help forestall disease. How can you dissolve accumulated, chronic reactions to either mildly or fiercely stressful events? One of the better ways to do this is to identify the tensions in your life. Identifying the major stresses in your life and then making new choices to deal with them may give you a leg up on stresses that could lead to disease.[16]

Make a list of the five greatest stresses in your life.

Check up on yourself; how are you taking part in supporting those stresses?

Think over ways you might remove those stresses. If it is not possible to take away tension or stress, ask whether you are fostering other nourishing essentials; e.g., maintaining friendships and allowing yourself "fun times" during stressful periods. Are you allowing yourself to talk about your stresses? Can you treat yourself better? Are you too hard on yourself?

What might happen to those stresses if you put your own needs first, even occasionally? Ask yourself, "What are my needs?" and "What are the needs of others that are mine to address?

Responses to a *JAMA* Article Debunking Therapeutic Touch

The beginner looking on may not be able to note the distinctions between Therapeutic Touch, Healing Touch, and Healing Hover Touch. Practitioners would know the difference, but they tend to look for similarities and do not concern themselves with the differences. When one of these disciplines is rebuked, all are rebuked. With permission, I draw heavily on Dr. Cynthia Poznanski-Hutchison's article,[17] published in response to the article (I would not classify it as a monograph) that appeared in the April 1, 1998, *Journal of the American Medical Association (JAMA).*[18] Since *JAMA* was *attempting* to debunk Therapeutic Touch and Dr. Poznanski Hutchison's response is so thorough, I include much of that response in this chapter.

First, I shall summarize the article to which this response was written. Two adults provided a literature search of materials written by practitioners and other proponents of Healing Touch and Therapeutic Touch. One of the researchers involved was Ms. L. Rosa, a nurse-ombudswoman, and the other was Mr. L. Sarner, an ombudsman. A physician assisted in writing the article. The fourth involved in the research (but not in the literature search) was Ms. E. Rosa, the nine-year-old daughter of Ms. L. Rosa.

The articles and monographs reviewed spanned the years 1972–96. The authors' primary criticism of the literature searched was in the experimental design being reported. All but one report of 853 reports was discounted, bringing the credibility and the significance of the studies into question. Nurses, many of whom are members of the American Holistic Nurses Association, authored many of the articles reviewed. Others reported research in master's theses and doctoral dissertations, and others were reported by physicians, some of whom oppose Therapeutic Touch, while still others are proponents of Therapeutic Touch. But please note the books and the thoroughly researched studies Poznanski-Hutchison suggests the researchers might wish to read, which they seemed to have missed in their search of the extant literature.

Also, I suggest reading Cohen[6] and Eisenberg,[15] as referred to in this book. I suggest this not because Cohen and Eisenberg are necessarily proponents of Therapeutic Touch or Qigong, but because of their open and thorough research into the efficacy and history of Qigong, the ancient Chinese precursor of Therapeutic Touch. Both Cohen and Eisenberg also relate numerous eyewitness accounts.

The statistical research undertaken by these four researchers was headed by the schoolgirl, who was actually conducting a school science fair project. As Poznanski-Hutchison points out in her review, the girl is the daughter of two people who oppose Therapeutic Touch. Experimenter bias might have led to negative results in the research.

The specific method used was to place the experimenter on one side of a screen with one of twenty-one subjects on the opposite side. The subject was asked to extend his or her hands through holes in the screen with the palms turned upward, approximately twelve inches apart. The subject's arms were draped to prevent peeking at which of their hands was closed to the hand of the experimenter.

The experimenter then held her hand about four inches

above one of the hands of the subject (which hand of the subject was determined by the toss of a coin). The experimenter would then indicate that the subject could say which hand he or she felt was in close proximity to the experimenter's hand. Each subject was tested several times and in two separate series. Twenty-one subjects in two trials, with a total of 280 attempts at identifying which of their own hands the hand of the experimenter was above, were correct 123 times, or 44 percent of the time. Pure chance would have given them 50 percent, which indicates that something in the experimental design was faulty or that there was experimenter bias.

Here I wish to share Poznanski-Hutchison's views and response (in italics), and I will interpolate more of my own later.

> Healing Touch is a program taught through the Colorado Center for Healing Touch in Lakewood, Colorado. It is a practitioner certification program endorsed by the American Holistic Nurses Association. In this program, we teach an eclectic blending of energetic techniques of a number of well-known healers, including Dolores Krieger's Therapeutic Touch as the foundationstone technique. Healing Touch is defined as a program which teaches the use of one's hands and intentionality to influence the health of another at physical, emotional, mental, and/or spiritual levels. A non-dogmatic approach is emphasized, focusing on intentionality of practitioner over technique, and inner development of the practitioner. Because we value the importance of scientific credibility, we also have an active research program to help answer the questions of how HT works and under what conditions. While we strive for a more scientific understanding of the energetic aspects of the human being, we simultaneously "embrace the mystery" of the person and the universe and accept that the answers may well come in their own time.

As a nurse researcher, psychotherapist, and Healing Touch practitioner and instructor, I offer these remarks based on the recent *Journal of the American Medical Association (JAMA)* article that claims to debunk Therapeutic Touch.

The published study does not test any critical variables related to Therapeutic Touch (TT). The ability to sense the energy field of another is simply not a requirement of a TT practitioner.

I started practicing TT fifteen years ago and used it for a few years before I began to sense energetically. Even now, I don't consider myself very kinesthetic, although this capacity has developed to some degree over time. I don't sense many of the things my beginning students do. So why did I keep on practicing? Because I could see that people I worked with were experiencing the relaxation response, pain relief, accelerated wound healing, mental clarity, emotional balance, and/or spiritual connection. What you do in your mind and heart far surpasses any kinesthetic experience in your hands. Being able to sense another person's energy is an aid in guiding one's treatment, but it is not an essential ingredient. Some practitioners sense a client's energy intuitively or are able to see or hear subtle aspects of the energy body (clairvoyance). Each person is unique in her or his abilities as a practitioner.

The study design was not representative of a Therapeutic Touch session.

It was set up more as a parlor game. Therapeutic Touch studies using people with health problems would most likely demonstrate positive effects.

The critical variables of practitioner compassion and holding the intentionality for the highest good of the recipient were not a part of the study. In the study setting, no healing was sought.

The child conducting the study was not neutral about Therapeutic Touch, and therefore could have affected the results.

The studies of Dan O'Leary at SUNY-Stony Brook have shown the "experimenter bias" effect, in which the beliefs of the experimenter tend to be confirmed. Controlled experiments look like they cannot possibly be affected by the experimenter's beliefs, but O'Leary showed that in the real world, they are. Emily has grown up in a household where she couldn't possibly be neutral about the existence of TT. Her thoughts may have blocked her own energy field from being perceived based on her belief that the practitioners could not be successful.

Practitioners are keenly aware of people's ability to block or close down their energy fields with their thoughts.

Healing Touch instructors usually demonstrate this phenomenon in introductory energy classes. Emily should have randomly chosen several classmates to participate who were not biased about the results, instead of herself.

Poznanski-Hutchison is correct in saying that "practitioners are keenly aware of people's ability to block or close down their energy fields with their thoughts." That is why I ask, sometimes several times, if a client is ready to let a condition go. (Review Chapter 4, "Instructions for Balancing Body Energy in Healing Hover Touch." And it is why more than a few times, the answer has been "No." They were not ready.

In addition, I agree that "Emily should have randomly chosen several classmates to participate who were not biased about the results, instead of herself." Another flaw in the experimental design was the determination to cut off any "air movement or body heat [that] might be detectable by the experimental subjects." They used an apparatus they tested that "prevented tactile cues from reaching the subject." That's the same as telling a surgeon that you want her to remove a tumor but that it must be done without the use of a scalpel.

In designing a more objective experiment, you would want more than just body heat to be the determining factor. If the researchers would choose totally unbiased experimenter assistants, they would witness an interesting phenomenon: Allow the healing touch practitioner to be in the position of the experimenter and the experimenter to be in the position previously occupied by the subject. The experimenters would not only identify which hand the practitioner's hand was above, but they would note a "tingling sensation," "intense tingling," "heat," "warmth," and myriad other descriptors. The experimenters could remain passive; i.e., not attempting to project Qi or body energy, or perhaps may even attempt to block the Qi, as appears may have been the case with the schoolgirl.

Allow the practitioner to take the proactive role of projecting energy. Choose experimenter assistants who truly know nothing about body energy or human energy fields and have no expectations. Allow them to describe what they are feeling instead of just using the binomial response of "my left hand" or "my right hand." They would need to be informed that they could say more than just one of these two answers—no suggestions about what they might say, just permission to talk. Identifying which hand could be given one-half a point and further description of extraordinary dimensions another one-half point. This type of experiment would get closer to a 75 to 80 percent accuracy, which is close to the percentage accuracy physicians achieve in their diagnoses, even with the help of sophisticated diagnostic equipment. Since clients/patients, subjects, and experimenters respond to identical sensations in various ways, requiring a 100 percent response rate is unreasonable. There are times when physicians misdiagnose just because a reticent patient is reluctant to share all their symptoms. An experimenter assistant, particularly a child, might be reluctant to share all the sensations their hands might feel.

Poznanski-Hutchison states further (with my comments in italics):

> The authors conclude that Therapeutic Touch is unscientific, but their claims that they have debunked Therapeutic Touch and rendered its use unjustified in the world of health care is not only unfounded and unscientific but unethical.
>
> *Theirs is one study which looked at one variable of the five steps of Therapeutic Touch, and it is the least critical of all variables/steps.*
>
> Dissecting Therapeutic Touch and claiming to disprove it by looking at a piece of it is like studying a horse by only looking at its legs. Their method was biased, unnatural, and fragmented. The five steps of Therapeutic Touch in clinical practice are done as a process and as a whole.
>
> The authors presented a piecemeal approach, which is adequate for a schoolgirl's science project. But Emily's study, which is only peripherally related to the actual practice of Therapeutic Touch, does not, as they claim, invalidate the professional practice and research of nurses over the last twenty-five years.
>
> *Studies since the early 1970s have progressively supported the use of Therapeutic Touch in the clinical setting.*
>
> Interestingly, the authors did not mention Wirth's (1992) TT study titled, "The Effect of Non-Contact

Therapeutic Touch on the Healing Rate of Full-Thickness Dermal Wounds." Wirth's study was randomized, double blind, and had a large subject size. Results strongly supported the use of TT in accelerating the rate of healing in full-thickness dermal wounds. Seminal controlled and blind studies were completed in the early 1960s by Bernard Grad, Sr. Justa Smith and others who studied the effect of the "laying on of hands" with plants, animals, and enzymes (which are not known to participate in the "placebo" effect). Their results were remarkable.

A final point is one of acknowledgement that there are many unanswered questions about energetic therapy!!

Practitioners know this and practice anyway because their experience has shown them phenomenal results. (Many practitioners also initially started out as strong skeptics.) Practitioners want to know more about "why, how, what if, and when?" and many are actively engaged in research. We don't have all the answers yet, and may never figure out every piece of the puzzle. However, while striving to understand energetic therapy from a scientific view, practitioners also "embrace the mystery" and let go of "the need to understand" during sessions. This is part of the beauty, awe, and humility that is experienced by many practitioners and patients.

Newton's theory in the 1600s described the human being as a divine type of mechanism or machine, with fixed parts, predictability, and alive within a closed system. But quantum physics of today describes us as fields within fields, as vibrating waves and particles, as equal to about two grains of sand in solid matter were we to be totally compressed. Modern physics supports the use of energetic therapy, most notably in the sentences: "Thought precedes form. Thought is a form of energy. Attention (presence) changes the object being observed." These statements directly relate to the intentionality that an energetic practitioner uses during treatments.

Spirituality and science have been kept separate since the scientific era, but more and more we are seeing the holism of all creation, the connectedness of everyone and everything, and the reemergence of science and spirituality as different perspectives of the same thing.

Studies on the existence of energy fields and the effects of energetic therapy have been published regularly since the practitioners have ignored, downplayed, or attacked a promising form of therapy to assist humanity in its suffering, healing, and dying.

The definition of a *skeptic* means "to be open-minded." I heartily implore anyone who is either against the use of energetic therapy or uninformed about it to explore it open-mindedly and fairly. Read *Vibrational Medicine* by Richard Gerber, M.D., or some of Deepak Chopra's books. Check out the *Medicine, Alternative and Complementary Therapies*, or *Subtle Energies* to become familiar with the research. Better yet, experience a short series of Therapeutic Touch, Healing Touch, or related energetic work with an open mind. Be skeptical if you like, but be open! (Since your thoughts are a part of you and your energy system, you can use them to block any positive effects.) Listen to the stories of people who have given and received the work. Then make your judgment.

We encourage solid research to study all aspects of

energetic healing in order to understand how it can best serve humanity. We invite healthy skepticism of all types of health care offered to society, mainstream and complementary.

We promote the study of natural, holistic, noninvasive, effective, and economical therapies, including the energetic therapies Therapeutic Touch, Healing Touch, and others. We desire to work alongside mainstream health care and provide the best of both worlds. We encourage consumers to educate themselves and be active in their personal health care and legislative decisions of the same.

After submitting this article to *JAMA*, my husband and I closely studied the statistics of Emily's study. Because the researchers don't believe in an energy field, they failed to consider the possibility that a lower than chance response from practitioners (50 percent) would be meaningful, which is exactly what happened. TT practitioners were correct only 42 percent of the time (combining the two studies), which is significantly lower than chance at the .05 level of significance using a two-tailed t-test (one out of twenty likelihood that the results were chance). If a one-tailed t-test is used in the negative direction, the significance is at the .025 level or one out of forty. We acknowledge the possibility that the results were "chance," and, of course, we recommend replication of the study (in a truer methodology). However, any statistician would conclude that, most likely, "something was happening" to make the results significantly lower than would be expected by chance in a binomial distribution (two possible responses: correct or incorrect). Therefore, we might hypothesize that the researchers' investment in a negative outcome is indeed what they created! It is possible/probable that the skeptics influenced the perception of the TT practitioners so that they were incorrect a majority of the time. In fact, with replication, it would be interesting to see if people who don't believe in energy fields may help to debunk their own belief.

Plans to replicate the *JAMA* study are in the works with Paul Mills, Ph.D., at UCSD Medical Center, and with Chris Wetzel, Ph.D., at Rhodes College in Memphis. Both studies will correct the methodology so that it more accurately reflects Therapeutic Touch.

I began this book in the first chapter by saying that the term *alternative medicine* is often threatening to both physicians and their patients. That's one reason, and a major one, that I prefer the term *integrative modalities of therapy.*

I am in favor of surgery when that is required. I favor the use of antibiotics if that is a *must.* I do not favor them for conditions that would respond to more natural means, even if the natural means takes longer to effect the cure. Overuse of antibiotics eventually renders them useless for people for whom antibiotics have been overprescribed. Additionally, new strains develop that are resistant to antibiotics.

My ideal for integrative therapies might be to have a physician who ordered x-rays because of a patient's back pain, who then reads them and sees her own limitations, and refers the patient to a chiropractor, who might also practice acupuncture. The chiropractor may then refer the patient to a nutritionist/exercise (or sports) trainer, who may help the patient over time to strengthen the back, minimizing the risk of future injury. It works the other way too: when a nutritionist recognizes that a condition requires medical treatment, he encourages the client to see a physician as soon as possible.

Researcher Eisenberg[15] said in 1995 that fair-minded research continues to lag behind the use of alternative therapies. In 1990, he and others at Beth Israel Hospital in Boston and Harvard

Medical School did a national survey to determine the types and frequency of the use of alternative therapy along with the amounts spent on them. Americans spent fourteen billion dollars on alternative (now variously called complementary or integrative) therapies, nearly eleven billion dollars of which was paid by the patient.

They further estimated that in that same year, Americans made 425 million visits to chiropractors, acupuncturists, homeopaths, energy healing practitioners, massage therapists, reflexologists, and other practitioners of integrative therapies. They concluded that this figure exceeded the number of calls on all internists, family practitioners, gynecologists, and pediatricians combined.

There are clinical reasons for the above findings. Alternative, complementary, integrative therapies are effective, and people are willing to pay for what works. The fact that Qigong and Therapeutic Touch border on being spiritual treatments is not a turnoff to clients. On the contrary, increasing numbers of patients see themselves as triune beings of spirit-mind-body, and they are stating openly in surveys and interviews that they wish their physicians would pray with them or at least discuss even briefly the value of faith in their healing process (see Chapter 12, and Mosley and Hill[19]). The population of the world (not just the United States) is increasing its awareness of and need for lifestyle changes that support regaining and maintaining wholeness. That awareness leads them to seek out the integrative modality of therapy they feel is right for their specific need.

Eisenberg[15] also shares one of his favorite Chinese proverbs: "Real gold does not fear even the hottest fire." That's true. Traditional Chinese medicine has nothing to fear from Qigong, nor does Qigong have anything to fear from traditional Chinese medicine. In fact, presidents of the traditional Chinese medical associations admit that they do not know exactly how Qigong works,[15] but they know that it does. It's hard to argue with three thousand years of success.

Nor do physicians of the Western cultures need to fear integrative modalities of therapy and vice versa. Qigong was in serious trouble for a few decades in the latter twentieth century, but as a result of politics, not because of opposition from the Chinese medical world.

I trust that Therapeutic Touch and other integrative healing systems will not experience the kind of efforts made for a few years by China's modern government to drive Qigong underground in the Western World. All of the integrative healing modalities have far too much to offer each other.

Pneumonia in Missouri and Cancer in the Dominican Republic

My maternal grandmother, Margaret "Meg" Headrick Wiseman Emerson, first told me this story during the summer I became fifteen years of age:

My mother, Viola Mildred "Millie" Wiseman, was born in November 1906 in a sharecropper's house; the house was located on a distant farm with a Cape Girardeau, Missouri, address, and it had no indoor plumbing and paper on the unfinished interior wall to cover the cracks in the vertical siding. In February 1907, Viola became ill with pneumonia and developed a dangerous fever. My grandfather, Jim Wiseman, rode on horseback the long distance into the Cape to ask the town-and-country doctor to come and visit his infant daughter.

Dr. Warburton visited and, with no antibiotics, did what he could for the baby. It became the typical fever watch that surrounded pneumonia in those days—watching and waiting, day and night, for the critical turning point. The only question on anybody's mind and heart was "*When* will" or "*Will* the fever ever break?" In 1907, much of the infant mortality in southeast

Missouri was a result of pneumonia. The doctor guessed that the fever might break within seventy-two hours (three full days).

Among those on the fever vigil was a black woman whose parents had been slaves. She was a young mother and a neighbor. When she discovered that my grandmother was also ill and unable to care for herself or for the baby, Lucille Jackson (Lucy, as she liked to be called) brought her own baby and cared for my grandmother and mother for several days.

Day after long night after long day came and went, and there was no change in the baby's condition. Finally, after five full days (during which the doctor had been unable to return), Lucy told my grandmother that she wanted to try a home remedy her mother and grandmother had shown her. Lucy began the treatment in the evening, and by early morning, my mother's fever had broken.

When the doctor finally returned, he examined the baby and asked when the fever had broken. My grandmother told him, "Only just this morning, and it was thanks to God, and to Lucy's efforts through the night."

Dr. Warburton asked Lucy what she had done, and she said, "I rubbed the baby's chest with olive oil all night." The doctor said that he had no idea that olive oil had healing properties.

My part-Cherokee grandmother, aware of folk remedies and always eager to learn more, laughed whenever she told this part of the story. She would say, "Lucy said, 'Why, Doctor, I'm s'prised at you! Olive oil don't have no healin' properties. The olive oil only kept me from irritatin' the baby's skin. It was love what done the healin.'"

Later, my mother became a nurse, and I had occasion to watch her place her hand on a feverish brow or hold a patient's hand. I've seen patients raise their heads off the pillow, and I've seen them put their hand on top of hers so that she couldn't take her hand away.

Back then, as a young adult, I figured these patients were rising up like a kitten that wants to get closer in order to be petted just because she was my mother. And it's true that my mother was a wonderful caregiver. Since that time, however, I have seen many, many patients respond similarly to many other hands-on caregivers.

It often seems that caregivers take their healing touch abilities for granted. While it is true that others can learn to use their inherent healing abilities as well, the hands-on caregivers definitely have a head start in developing this capacity for helping others.

En La Republica Dominicana

After a six-hour workshop (i.e., three hours, plus translation) with approximately three hundred people in Santo Domingo, most of the students wanted to stay to see what a healing treatment would "feel like" from the instructor (*me!*), as well as from those who had been their practice partners during the workshop. Besides the Dominican Republic, attendees had come from Mexico, Ecuador, the United States, Colombia, Venezuela, Puerto Rico, and Costa Rica. Many had no presenting complaints, but they were eager students. And, as usual, still others had come because of serious healing needs.

One man came with advanced abdominal cancer. With help, he was still ambulatory. He had had extensive surgery and chemotherapy, and a minimal amount of radiation therapy. He came to the weeklong program (during which there were other presentations) with particular abdominal pain, a generalized discomfort, and a very gloomy prognosis—that is, there was no known way to do anything more for him.

But Manuel (as I shall call him) was gutsy and not ready to quit.

Through our mutual friend and the workshop translator, (the *now* Reverend) Xiomara Malagon, we talked. Manuel gave me a brief history, and I began to work with him. I started with a general balancing of his body energy and an assessment.

If I were a physician, as was noted previously, the assessment might be called a diagnosis. When I make an assessment, I'm attempting three tasks simultaneously: First, I'm looking for physical limitations of which the client may not be aware. Second, I am using energy in an effort to assist the client. Third, I'm looking for wellness in the client's body, which I can use to assist me in balancing the client's body energy. When it is necessary I also visualize, or envision, greater health than presently appears to be manifest.

After I made a complete pass over Manuel's body from head to foot in front and I had just begun to balance the energy at the top of his head and the back of his neck, he sighed a great sigh. He told us it was as though the generalized discomfort throughout his body had just lifted, like a fog. Although his abdomen still had some discomfort, it no longer had the "red" pain he had lived with for eighteen months or so—except during periods when he was heavily medicated in the hospital.

The next morning, Manuel told me that at about 4:00 a.m. he had had his first unassisted bowel movement in several months.

Manuel was a widower and was attending the Personal Growth Week activities with a cousin. The two men had been practice partners the day before. So, twice that day, I worked with the cousin on what to look for (more accurately, what to feel for, or to sense) in his non-touch practice with Manuel.

Manuel's cousin (whom I shall call Juan Ricardo) described himself as wanting to help Manuel, but also as "unwilling to attend, unable to learn 'woo-woo' techniques." Even if everybody else could use them, he was sure he would be unable to use them.

With little more instruction than being shown what to do physically and some demonstration as to what he would feel, Juan Ricardo began treating Manuel. With his eyes closed, Manuel had a halcyon look.

Back home in my office a few months later, I received a letter from Manuel. He wrote that, with no other treatment except that of his cousin doing Healing Hover Touch, he had returned to his oncologist for verification that he was clean of cancer.

Since all I want to see happen is for people to get well, I suggest as many ways to regain health as I am aware of. During the fall 1987 class that Manuel and Juan Ricardo attended, I mentioned (and then later reaffirmed personally to them) that use of *Pau D'Arco* tea (available in health food stores) had had beneficial effects for many cancer patients whom I knew. I encouraged them to use both the tea and Healing Hover Touch. These integrative modalities of treatment can work simultaneously. It does not need to be either/or, but can be both/and.

In his letter, however, Manuel told me that he had been unable to get Taheebo tea (also known as *Pau D'Arco* and *Ipe Roxo*). Since the work with his cousin was benefiting him so much, he did not pursue acquiring the tea. Manuel added that his cousin sent his apology for calling these healing techniques "woo-woo" just because he didn't understand them.

Perhaps a few added thoughts here will help. In 1987, the bulk bark of the *Pau D'Arco* tree (this is splintered bark; the bark grows back after two years) was strong enough so that most people who used it successfully as a treatment for cancer were able to do so with just three cups of tea per day. Now, just after the turn of the century, those who have used it successfully say that it is necessary to drink six to nine cups daily.

The explanation for the difference is that the strongest tea is made from the bark of trees grown on the top of mountains (in the ozone layer) in central South America. To meet increasing world demands for the tea, it has been necessary to mix in bark from the mid-mountain trees as well as from those that grow at the lowest mountain levels.

The tea's common name, Taheebo tea, derives from the South American native tribe who has used it as their only drink for many centuries. When they are weaned from mother's milk (which, of course, contains Taheebo tea), these natives begin drinking Taheebo tea.

As we begin this new century and millennium, more and more cancer patients are using IP-6 (inositol hexaphosphate)[20]—which is also available in health food stores—in addition to, and sometimes instead of, Taheebo tea.

Please note that none of the above strategies or products used successfully by others is to replace other medical care, but are to be used in addition to it. Just as allopathic medicine and chiropractic adjustment may complement each other and increase the benefit to the patient, and as chiropractic and nutritional therapy may work together, so may Healing Hover Touch, Therapeutic Touch, Reiki, and Feldenkrais work with each other, as well as with nutritional therapy and acupuncture.

As it relates to increasing cooperation in science and spirituality, Templeton[21] astutely observes that when groups with any cause—sacred or secular—start to believe that they have all the answers, the movement ceases to move and essentially calcifies.

Similarly, regarding cooperation and patient/client confidence, Weil[22] quotes one of his patients: "There may be different ways to healing for different people but there is always a way. Keep searching!"

For me, this idea is essential. If you come to the end of what help seems to be available by one of the modalities of treatment, try again. Study the research, inquire of knowledgeable people in the field, and try the next most likely method for making progress toward healing, if that is possible; seek at least greater comfort, if not healing. Second, third, and more opinions might also mean second, third, and more modalities of treatment.

Like life itself, healing practices are lived forward but are understood backward. Looking backward, having come as far as we have in the latter twentieth and the early twenty-first centuries, it will be good if the conductors of healing—those currently practicing integrative modalities of treatment—don't settle into believing now that *they* have *the way* of health, healing, and wholeness. We need to include all modalities: acupuncture, allopathy, bodywork, chiropractic, Healing Touch, Healing Hover Touch, laying on of hands, massage therapy, Qigong, surgery, vitamin therapy, yoga, and at least one hundred more.

Since life is lived in a context of relationships, and since the most significant ones impact our physical, emotional, and spiritual beings so pervasively, we consider them in the next two chapters.

CHAPTER NINE

Reciprocal Health and Well-Being of Household Pets and Their Humans

Statistics are staggering regarding the numbers of households that have at least one dog or cat. Add to that the numbers of birds, turtles, mice, and ferrets, as well as the numbers of exotic birds, snakes, iguanas, and other pets, and we average at least one pet per household in the United States. There is a reason for that. People look to these little ones for companionship, often even with a house full of people. Sometimes, people in the family don't even consider the pet as a *family* pet. Each may think of it as *my* pet. Most of these pets want something of a relationship, too.

Regarding the selection of a dog as a pet, Campbell, Thornton, and Fortney[23] observed, "Dogs are smart, social animals, so no matter what kind of dog you get, he'll want and need to spend quality time with you." Certainly the same can be said for practically all pets. It surely is true of my family's four Boston terrier lightweights, the late Princess Narwhal (named from the image of a white Narwhal whale emblazoned on the back of her neck, which was otherwise black) and her sister, the late Princess Chelsea. We now share the lives of Princess Annabelle and

Princess Hannah May, also Boston terriers. One of the reasons we have chosen to have two dogs is because my wife and I work very long days, so they have each other for company when we are not around, and the four of us have each other when we are around.

Many retirement communities that previously prohibited pets of any kind (though many residents sneaked in parakeets or gerbils as substitutes for a cat or dog) are now encouraging retirees to bring their pets with them when they move in. If the pet dies, restrictions no longer prevent the residents from getting another. There is a reason for this, too. Seniors who have pets generally tend to remain healthier than those who do not have pets, and the people usually remain happier and are therefore more pleasant tenants. This is particularly true for those retirees who do not have human companionship.

Like for people, it is important for pets to have good and appropriate nutrition, usually not food from the dining table. Steak may be good for blood type O humans (refer to information in Chapter 10, "Eat Right 4 Your (Blood) Type: A Book Review"), but not necessarily for all domesticated dogs or cats. Small dogs may not even do well with chicken from the table, especially not commercially raised chicken. The excess fat is difficult for a small dog to assimilate.

Anyone who has ever had a beloved pet who became sick knows how much one may agonize until the little one is returned to health. I refer to the father-and-son team of veterinarians whom we take our "girls" to as their "pediatricians." That is a reflection of how I feel about my two princesses. I know I'm not unique; I know many other people who are also owned by their pets and feel similarly.

Many people who have been faced with a one thousand dollar veterinary bill, or even two thousand dollars for tests or surgery, don't blink an eye—not because they're wealthy, but because they care for the pet so much. Suddenly, money is no object. One veterinarian recently noted that sometimes friends and relatives criticize a pet owner for spending $2,200 on a beloved pet, which they will enjoy for years to come. On the other hand, the critic may well spend $22,000 on a boat that they put on a lake and perhaps visit once in a while. Neither is right or wrong. We just do what is important to us to do.

And sometimes, as in the case of people, there is not enough money in the world to help a pet get well, because the prognosis is not very bright. That's when love and loving caretaking, just as in the case of people who are traumatically ill, are the primary building blocks for a return to health.

The True Story of Artie's Healing

A friend and colleague, the Reverend Dawna Roberts (her recently acquired last name is Mantei), tells the story of her dog, Artie, and Artie's "pediatrician." Notice the surprise ending to the story that follows.

> About six years ago I began considering going into ministry. However, I had some doubts about some of our teachings, and healing was one of those doubts. Since healing is such a big part of Unity's belief system, I felt I could not apply for ministerial school until I received a new understanding, so I prayed and released the entire consideration to God. I gave myself permission to doubt whatever I needed to while still leaving an opening for proof. I truly released it.
>
> Approximately at the same time, our dog groomer noticed a lump on a hind leg of my little dog, Artie. I took him to his veterinarian (Glenn calls her Artie's pediatrician) and she took a biopsy and sent it to a lab for evaluation. The report was that Artie had cancer. I was really devastated; this little Schnauzer was a *huge* chunk of my world.
>
> A few weeks after the cancer diagnosis, I was on my treadmill when a new experience began happening. I wasn't praying, meditating, or even thinking about God that I can remember, when suddenly a feeling of intense love began pouring through me. It felt as though someone took the top of my head off

and poured liquid love through my entire body.

At first I thought I might have had a heart attack or something else and that I was actually dying. Then I asked myself, "Where is the white light?" I got off the treadmill, and it was as though everything in the room was *alive* and I *loved all of it.* This experience is very difficult to explain because I don't think there are words to explain it. I was experiencing the kind of love, I think, that people talk about when they have a near-death experience, except that I was very much alive.

Artie was lying on his back on my bed with his little legs all sprawled out and the lump, which had grown quite large by this time, was popped out and in full view. What I remember most about this whole thing is that I walked over and put my hand on the lump and I could feel nothing but love for it. I apologized to it for hating and resenting it, and at some intuitive level, I knew it had intelligence and was receiving my love.

From start to finish, the entire experience lasted about six hours. After that, life went on as before but I was changed at depth. I had experienced God's love, a kind of *super* love that was beyond definition or description.

When Artie and I went for walks together, the lump became noticeably larger, but a calm peace had replaced my devastation. I knew without a doubt that Artie was made of love and that love never dies and he would go on to a greater experience of God when his time came. I also knew I would be comforted when it happened. It wasn't long until the lump was so large that his leg would stick out as he walked.

A month or so after the treadmill experience I went to Costa Rica to do volunteer work for two weeks. When I returned home, I picked Artie up to hug him. I would hold him like a baby, on his back, in my arms. As I held him I looked down for the lump, but it was gone—completely gone.

My initial reaction was one of fear and devastation and I began to cry and I said to my late husband, "David, now his cancer has burst and it's going through his whole body."

David was a physician and he responded, "That can't be; it was a hard, cancerous tumor. It can't burst." David checked him over carefully and said that we'd better see Dr. Williams.

Dr. Williams could not believe her eyes either, so she retrieved the biopsy reports and re-verified Artie's condition. Then she took another biopsy to be sure, and this time the report indicated that Artie was clean of cancer.

Artie was healthy as a horse ... or a Schnauzer. Completely healed. And so was I.

I knew intuitively that through the love of God, anything and anyone could be healed. I may not understand how it happens, but I understand that it does. And that's enough for me.

Three months later Dr. Williams called me, which threw me into great fear. I was afraid she might be calling to say that the "clean" biopsy report was in error. She asked if I would come to see her in her office. I asked whether I should bring Artie and she said that wasn't necessary. Since our only relationship revolved around Artie, I was really concerned.

Once I was seated in her office, Dr. Williams asked me exactly what had happened with Artie and how he was healed. She asked me what I did and for any other details I thought were important. I told her the events described above as well and as accurately as I could.

When I finished, she was quiet for a good length

of time. Finally she said, "I have an inoperable and otherwise untreatable tumor. My prognosis for both quality and length of life is not good. I am an agnostic, so I do not pray, but does it count that I believe in reincarnation of animals, and that I love animals?"

[Author's note: the belief of most of the Asian religions and many in the rest of the world that animals return to life on earth repeatedly is a belief in transmigration of spirit, not reincarnation. Reincarnation relates only to humans.]

I told her that the love she had for animals (and I knew she had great love for her family as well) was a good place to begin because love is another name for God.

She asked what I thought she might do. I suggested that she begin by loving the tumor. I told her that before the experience with Artie, I hated the tumor and said so aloud. I would envision little Pacmen eating the cancer cells, but I don't believe in hating the cancer anymore and I don't see anything eating the cells.

I told her that I had come to love the cells and the tumor and that I had said so aloud. I spoke directly to the tumor as I put my hands on it. So I told her to do the same thing with her tumor, to put her hand over it, to love the tumor and to say so aloud.

Dr. Williams said, "I don't think I can do that." Since she was agnostic and didn't pray, I had nothing else to tell her and I told her that.

Eventually she decided to try it. She said she began by telling the tumor that she loved it with her hand over the site. Next, she brought her blood reports and the MRI pictures into the equation. She developed a relationship with the diseased cells and told them specifically that she loved them. To shorten what could be a long story, it worked.

Artie lived to be seventeen years old, six years past his bout with cancer, and three days past the opening of the doors of my new church. Dr. Williams was still his "pediatrician" and was with him when he died.

Summing Up Artie's Story

Dawna made several excellent points in telling a story that involves two such important "people" in her life, and I want to reiterate one: "I may not understand how it happens, but I understand that it does. And that's enough for me."

Praying people—especially, perhaps, metaphysicians—have often prayed to make good things appear in their lives and bad things disappear, and when the desired result comes about, often they have concluded that they did it themselves, or at the very least, act as though they understood what happened. Sometimes I think we may not know, but we may have an inkling as to how miracles occur. But most of the time, personally, I'm with Dawna on this one. I don't understand *how* it happens, only *that* it happens. And that's enough for me, too.

Even though we may not know how healing occurs, our prayers are answered. Now we continue our search in the next chapter. We seek our own healthful practices by looking at what we eat, how we prepare what we eat, and—as I have alluded to a couple of times already—how it may be related to our individual blood types.

CHAPTER TEN

Eat Right 4 Your Type—A Book Review

Dr. Peter D'Adamo has developed an individualized diet solution to staying healthy while living longer and being able to achieve ideal body weight; he has described his plan in his best-selling book, *Eat Right 4 Your Type: The Individualized Diet to Staying Healthy, Living Longer, and Achieving Your Ideal Weight.*[24]

In medicine and psychology, as well as in spiritual counseling, practitioners are reminded to never treat two people with the same methods. Yet much of what is recommended all over the world to people who are ill and, specifically, overweight appears to be cookie-cutter advice.

One diet suggests a high intake of protein, and the next suggests a high intake of carbohydrates. Another suggests the right ratio of protein to carbohydrates to fats. Usually, the first two recommend a low intake of fats. The assumption seems to be that if one simply loses weight that they are then likely to be healthy—one size fits all.

If that were true, everyone could memorize the one right plan for healthy living (and there would only be one plan) and follow it, and all would be healthy and maintain an appropriate weight.

Dr. D'Adamo built his own research of fifteen years onto the thirty years of work done by his father, who is also a naturopathic physician. Their work demonstrates that the four ABO (O, A, B, and AB) blood types are central to understanding which foods help in maintaining and regaining health, as well as the ones that help in attaining and maintaining an appropriate weight.

Dr. D'Adamo presents evidence that the development of blood types is related to food sources around the world—not just in the past ten thousand to twenty-five thousand years, but, in the case of Type O, over the past several hundred thousand years. Generally, the foods that fit your blood type are the foods that predominated at the time in history when your blood type first appeared.

Certain foods can assist the strengths to which we are predisposed and minimize inherent potential weaknesses according to our blood types. Some foods help people with certain blood types; the same foods may be deleterious to health in people of different blood types. By emphasizing and ingesting the foods that help and by eliminating those foods that are wholly antagonistic, you can foster the most beneficial balance for your digestive and immune systems. I predict that the information in this book will be some of the most important work in medicine in the twenty-first century.

Quoting from the Book's Dust Jacket

In *Eat Right 4 Your Type*, D'Adamo shows:

- Which foods, spices, teas, and condiments help someone of your blood type maintain optimal health and ideal weight

- Which vitamins and supplements to emphasize or avoid

- Which medications function best in your system

- Whether your stress goes to your muscles or your nervous system

- Whether your stress is relieved better through aerobics or meditation

- Whether you should walk, swim, or play tennis or golf as your mode of exercise

- How knowing your blood type can help you avoid many common viruses and infections

- How knowing your blood type can help you fight back against life-threatening diseases

- How to slow down the aging process by avoiding factors specific to your blood type that cause rapid cell deterioration

As important as I think this book by Dr. D'Adamo is for every adult, it is at least equally important for children (and grandchildren). I believe this book is potentially a life-extender for most anyone who reads it and follows its advice. For me, that means the earlier in life, the better. My wife and I have given copies of the book to our grown children with encouragement to get our grandchildren on their blood-type diets.

The need to get this message into the hands of children draws to mind a moment in time several of us shared with Dr. D'Adamo, Martha, his wife, and their two young daughters.

——(o)——

A couple of years ago, an honored friend, mentor, and colleague of both Dr. D'Adamo's and mine, the Reverend Eric Butterworth of New York City, passed away. Dr. D'Adamo and I were deeply honored to be two of the speakers at the memorial service.

Afterwards, we went to a luncheon arranged by Mrs. Olga Butterworth. Because of my long-avowed admiration and support of Dr. D'Adamo and his work, she arranged for us to sit together. Martha D'Adamo and their children sat directly across from me.

It was a delight to watch and to listen to the two young daughters discuss with their parents and—even more significantly to me, with each other—what they would order that would work with their blood types.

How very fortunate for these two young ladies that they are so far ahead in maintaining their health so early in their lives.

Since my first reading of *Eat Right 4 Your Type* in early 1997, I have been following and benefiting from its guidance myself. I have recommended it in my healing workshops and have encouraged sponsors of my workshops (whether religious or medical) to have copies of the book available for purchase. I've heard from students in distant places of how grateful they are that I pointed them in the direction of this book.

I encourage you to read the book, *Eat Right 4 Your Type*, and its recently published (1998) kitchen companion, *Cook Right 4 Your Type: The Practical Kitchen Companion to Eat Right 4 Your Type*. May both volumes become well-worn from use as manuals on healthy eating and healthy lifestyles.

A Brief Introduction to the Author of Eat Right 4 Your Type

Noted naturopathic physician Dr. Peter J. D'Adamo is a thoroughgoing researcher and publisher-lecturer of his discoveries. His clinical testing of the connection of blood type to health and disease has led to groundbreaking work with several illnesses, including breast cancer. Dr. D'Adamo was selected Physician of the Year in 1990 by The American Association of Naturopathic Physicians, and Clinician of the Month for February 1991 by *Preventive Medicine Update*. He has a flourishing practice in Stamford, Connecticut, and he is the founder and editor emeritus of *The International Journal of Naturopathic Medicine*.

CHAPTER ELEVEN

My Experience with Chelation Therapy

For several years, I ran for fitness and recreation, and I even participated in long-distance (endurance) races. One spring as I began training, I experienced chest pains for several days consecutively. Although I had lived in the area for five years, I had no physician.

I inquired and made an appointment with a general practitioner. He examined me; among other tests, he did an electrocardiogram (EKG). He concluded that I was healthy and that my heart was singularly healthy. When I consider the personal upheaval my life was in at the time, I'm sure the doctor was right. I was healthy—and I had earned the right to have chest pains, even with a healthy heart. However, because I wanted to continue running, I asked for a prescription to take an athlete's stress test at a local hospital. The G.P. suggested instead that I should stop running.

Nonetheless, he gave me the prescription. My stress test appointment was early Monday morning, June 23, 1980. I quickly learned the difference between an athlete's stress test and a regular treadmill test. I was duly connected to the monitor, with a nurse on each side, both with blood pressure cuffs on my arms. Throughout the test, the stress lab head physician stayed close as well.

They asked me to get the stationary bicycle up to twenty-five miles per hour and to keep it there for ten minutes while one of the nurses periodically added hydraulic pressure weights. She would warn me when she was about to add weights, and I would run the bike up to over thirty miles per hour. Then she would add the weights, and that would drag the speed back down to twenty-five miles per hour. Both nurses commented they had never seen anyone do this so well (and my blood pressure was great)! Usually, the test subject would be warned that weights were being added, then the weights were added, and the speed was dragged down to twenty miles per hour. The subject would then spend the next minute trying to get back to twenty-five miles per hour.

The test lab physician commented after the test that he had attended more than ten thousand stress tests and he had seen people try to stay ahead of the weights before, but this was one of the best-executed tests he had ever seen.

Eight minutes after the test was over, I went into cardiac arrest. Lest you conclude from this that I had a heart attack, I hasten to add that I did not. A heart attack leaves heart muscle damage; I had no heart muscle damage. In retrospect, this would have been a really good time to remember that the examining general practitioner reaffirmed several times that he envied the health of my heart.

However, I was placed in the cardiac care unit for one day and then transferred to the cardiac wing the next day.

After I was out of the cardiac care unit, a friend whom I had not seen for several months called me. Larry was a forty-two-year-old Ph.D. psychologist who had had triple bypass surgery during the last week of December 1979 (six months earlier). By late April, the bypass was breaking down and he faced another surgical procedure. In view of the apparent failure of my friend's surgery, this was not a welcome notion.

An acquaintance of his suggested he consider chelation therapy. After Larry investigated chelation, he decided to try it. He had had tests to determine whether chelation could help his condition. Between May 1 and June 25, he had had about twenty treatments. He was well satisfied; all symptoms indicating that he might need new surgery were totally cleared by the fifteenth treatment (and acknowledged by the surgeon who had told him that he needed a second surgery). He had begun feeling the return of the energy that he had had a year before.

Let me digress just enough to give you at least an operational definition of chelation (*key-lay-shun*) therapy, and a few personal observations.

Chelation is a system of therapy in which a synthetic amino acid called ethylene diamine tetra-acetic acid (EDTA) is administered intravenously. Chelation must be prescribed by and supervised by either an osteopathic or allopathic physician. In the American College for Advancement in Medicine information pamphlet, "Chelation Therapy: New Hope for Victims of Arteriosclerosis and Age-Associated Diseases,"[25] states, "The fluid containing EDTA is infused through a small needle placed in the vein of a patient's arm. The EDTA in solution bonds with metals in the body and carries them away in the urine. Abnormally situated nutritional metals, which speed free radical damage, and toxic metals, such as lead, are most easily removed by EDTA."

The procedure may require from thirty to fifty treatments in the first several weeks, and then generally the patient may take one per month. (For more information, write to the American College for Advancement in Medicine address in Appendix A.)

Although approval of the treatment by the U.S. Food and Drug Administration (FDA) is primarily for lead poisoning and not for arteriosclerosis (hardening of the arteries), I have read several books and well over one hundred articles and monographs on chelation, and I have had more than two hundred treatments. A few years ago, I had an echocardiogram and, along with the technician, I watched the pumping of my heart from the inside. The technician, an employee of a hospital who knew nothing about my chelation treatments, said, "Oh, look at that heart. It's as pure and clean as a newborn baby's heart." When I asked her if she would like to know how that happened to be so, she said that she would like to know.

I told her that I had taken chelation therapy for the previous twelve years. She responded with, "Oh." That was the end of the conversation.

———(o)———

Let's return now to my first introduction to chelation therapy by my psychologist friend, Larry.

Larry's opening words were, "Glenn, I've just learned that you are in cardiac care and I'm calling to tell you good news; don't let them do a catheterization on your heart and don't let them cut on you." I asked for the rest of his good news.

I asked visiting friends who were nurses to check out whatever they could find in the library about chelation therapy and to bring it in and read it to me (I was too fatigued to hold a book up).

On Thursday evening, two administrative nurses came to ask me to sign the permission to perform catheterization on my heart on Friday morning. When I asked why it was necessary, the spokesperson said that it was so they would know where to do the surgery on Monday morning.

I told her that it appeared they had found my heart guilty and it hadn't yet had a trial. We talked awhile longer, and I told the two nurses that I was going to check out in the morning and I was going to see a medical doctor near my home who was a chelation therapist and acupuncturist. Saying not one word more, both nurses beat a speedy retreat from my room.

Within a half hour or so, I faced an awesome sight in my room. The two nurses returned with an additional nurse (my primary caregiver on that shift) and five physicians. Included were the chief cardiologist (who was my neighbor), a doctor on hospital staff, the stress lab chief physician, the chief physician who was in doing rounds, and a fifth person—who seemed to be there just to reinforce the efforts of the other seven medical personnel, in the event I should resist too strongly, I would guess.

The eight of them carried on a somewhat brisk conversation

on the pros of their suggested procedure (never mentioning whether there were any cons), and all the cons on chelation therapy (never mentioning whether there were any pros). The general practitioner told me he would not check me out. When I told them that I would check myself out of the hospital in the morning to go see the chelation therapist, the chief cardiologist gave the final word as they left my room: "When you do, you'll leave the hospital, step off the curb, and be dead before you hit the pavement."

I am sometimes accused of seizing a blinding glimpse of the obvious, and perhaps it doesn't need to be articulated, but I feel the need to say it anyway: "That is a lot of pressure per square inch on anybody." I lay in that hospital bed questioning whether what I was doing was right, but actually I could only say that it felt right for me.

About twenty minutes after the entourage left me alone, my primary caregiver nurse for that evening put her head around the corner of my room, smiled broadly at me, gave me a thumbs-up gesture, and departed; her shift was over. I checked out of the hospital the next morning (actually, the G.P. who gave me the test prescription returned and, without coming to see me a final time, wrote the release for me). I never saw the nurse again. I was never certain whether the thumbs-up was saying, "Good for you; you're doing the right thing," or "Good luck; you're going to need it."

A friend took me to the medical doctor who practiced chelation and acupuncture. She put me through several tests in the morning, and I took my first treatment in the afternoon.

I returned to a full work schedule (basically that was sixty-plus hours weekly) within two weeks. After six weeks, I called the G.P. who had kindly written the stress test prescription for me and asked him for the hospital's final test results as to why I had the cardiac arrest—since my heart was verified and reverified to be healthy. At first, he told me hospital records were confidential, but eventually he agreed to send a copy to me.

The bottom line was that my electrolytes were out of balance; specifically, my potassium level was low. While I was running, I always ate what I thought were enough raisins—but apparently, this time, I didn't eat quite enough.

How You Can Help Health Professionals to Treat You Beyond Prescriptions

From my interactions with tens of thousands whom I have taught and who have taught me in Healing Hover Touch classes, medical in-service and multi-media presentations and interactive learning experiences (classes and workshops), I have found that people are increasingly eclectic in their pursuit of health and wholeness, as well as in their pursuit of other complex interests.

While no two people necessarily describe their health needs in exactly the same—or even similar—terms, what health-care professionals need to know is the rate at which patients are turning to integrative systems of treatment (see Eisenberg[15] and Chapter 7, "Responses to a *JAMA* Article Debunking Therapeutic Touch"). It is also valuable to note that Eisenberg and colleagues in two institutions have founded a center for researching alternative medicine, "under the joint aegis of Beth Israel Hospital and Harvard Medical School."

In an awakening world, more and more people tend to no longer take over-the-counter or prescription medications without finding out what their effects are first. Exceptions might include short-term use of analgesics for pain relief or antibiotics to treat infection.

> In a random sample of 160 family physicians in Illinois, we found that about one-third of physicians prayed with their elderly patients; the vast majority of physicians indicated prayer was helpful "somewhat" (33.9 percent) or "a great deal" (55.4 percent).
>
> —*Koenig, Bearon, and Dayringer*[26]

A significant portion of the general population seems to have an inherent belief that spontaneous healing is possible and that they have a vested interest in not over-providing external help. Further, many are inclined to look to modalities of treatment other than, or in addition to, medication or surgery.

Next we look at some very simple actions to take to provide one's body with appropriate assistance and not rely so much on external help. Try exploring some of these techniques.

Nutrition, Breathing, Physical Exercises, and Meditation in Health and Well-Being

As I noted in the previous section, people are increasingly eclectic in their pursuit of health and well-being. They tend to read, study, and experiment with myriad ways to promote good health. Further, more than 50 percent of those participating in healing interactive learning experiences I facilitate indicate that they participate in physical exercise at least minimally (one to six times a week, fifteen to forty-five minutes each time).

Physical exercises and spiritual disciplines that include a physical component most often mentioned include brisk walking (outside or treadmill), stair-climbing (actual stairs or on a machine), swimming, golfing, low-impact aerobics, hiking, stationary or moving bicycling, skiing (outside or machine), yoga, and martial arts. Some small percentage actually practice relaxation techniques, nutrition approaches, breathing exercises, and meditation, while others have at least read about or heard reports in the media on the benefits of these techniques. The study and practice of *pranayama*, an ancient East Indian breath control practice that is a part of yoga, is at once an authentic spiritual discipline and one of the pathways to regaining and maintaining good health. A health-care professional might well work with the patient/client and prescribe a varying combination of these activities.

A precautionary word is appropriate here. It seems self-evident that it is important that we look vigilantly for the variety of regimens we may follow to maintain health and wholeness for our families and ourselves. It is at least equally important to seek diligently to identify those behaviors we engage in and products we consume that we may want to change or eliminate.

In this next section, I introduce two books that provide important information. In my opinion, the first—on ways to prevent, treat, and even reverse Alzheimer's—has no peer. The second is one of the best books of its type—it is filled with suggested home remedies for a myriad of conditions.

The Link Between Alzheimer's and Fluoridated Water

There are more than fifty identified causes[27] that appear to impact the functioning of the brain and lead to dementia. Those causes include the following (the short list): pharmaceuticals (prescribed and recreational), neurotoxins (aspartame and glutamate), genetic and environmental factors, Parkinson's disease, allergies, syphilis, brain tumors, heavy metals (specifically, aluminum and lead), alcohol, and sodium fluoride. The most common form of advanced dementia is Alzheimer's disease.

Fluoridation of drinking water, which has been closely tied to Alzheimer's, has ceased in most countries in the world except the United States and countries that are strongly influenced by the United States. Numerous highly respected scientists and scientific institutes (the Pasteur and Nobel Institutes among them) oppose water fluoridation, but it still continues.

Do not assume that what is being done in the name of health and well-being is actually good for you or others and, most especially, for children, the elderly, and those with health problems. A labor union representing scientists and engineers at the Environmental Protection Agency in Washington, D.C., opposes water fluoridation, but it still continues.

By standards of medicine in the Western world, reversing Alzheimer's is thought to be impossible. Treatment primarily comprises containment, support, and alleviating the symptoms. Books on Alzheimer's help families to accept the diagnosis, find support groups, and choose nursing facilities. Since it is believed that Alzheimer's cannot be reversed nor the brain damage repaired, no one before has tried to write a book discussing the reversal of the disease.

All of the books listed in the references and the suggested reading lists at the back of this book were selected for their value to the subject at hand: regaining and sustaining wholeness, and specifically the topics in this chapter. If you or someone you know is dealing with Alzheimer's disease in himself or in a loved one, consider Kathryn Picoulin's book, *Reversing Alzheimer's Naturally*[27] (see Appendix A for product source). Her book is full of how-to's in reversing this increasingly common disease, and her bibliography is also excellent. Picoulin's credentials are stellar: she is a nurse, a Ph.D., and a naturopathic physician, and she is responsible for reversing her father's Alzheimer's disease. She speaks from experience.

Much damage can be and is being done to children and adults long before Alzheimer's can set in. Numerous studies in China have proved fluoridation's negative effect, statistically as much as thirty points on the I.Q. of children.

The elderly and especially people with cardiovascular problems and diabetes must avoid sodium fluoride. They cannot excrete the fluoride sufficiently and are "more susceptible to fluoride toxicity. Pregnant women must also avoid sodium fluoride due to fluoride's ability to cross the blood brain barrier into the brain, especially into the brain of a developing fetus."[27] There is mounting evidence against poisoning our water supply with fluorides, and still it continues.

If your local water is being fluoridated, you may want to join a movement to get it stopped, or start the movement yourself. If it is not now being fluoridated, perhaps you might wish to join with others in making sure the practice does not get started. Consider whether or not you wish to allow fluoridation to continue where you live. You can effectively filter your own city drinking water *only* through a reverse osmosis system. Common household filters are useless, especially against fluorides, but even if we all use reverse osmosis to filter our water supply, fluoride will still be in practically every food product you buy—from liquids to bread and cereal. When health food store products say in the list of ingredients, "filtered water," it may mean the water has not undergone reverse osmosis and therefore contains fluorides. Essentially, we need to get the poisoning of our public water supplies stopped. Picoulin lists risk factors, dietary changes (listing specific beverages and foods to eliminate from your diet and ones to incorporate into your diet, pages 113–114[27]), and alternative/integrative remedies designed to correct, and means of prevention of, many of the fifty factors most commonly related to dementia. As Picoulin points out (page 5): "Ignorance is not bliss . . . Knowledge is."

A Good Source Book for Home Remedies

A second book, *God Helps Those Who Help Themselves*, by Hanna Kroeger[28] has particularly useful how-to's for home remedies to treat a number of maladies, from a toxic colon to stomach distress to lead poisoning and concerns around leukemia (see Appendix A for product information).

A Warning, Reiterated

Before we go further, let me say for the benefit of the nonprofessional reader or prospective patient/client who has not already studied and discovered alternatives to prescription drugs with possible undesired side effects, that one needs to exercise caution regarding self-diagnosis. While it is useful to listen to your body and mind to determine needs and courses of action, it cannot be overemphasized that it is also good to work with a health-care professional regarding the use of nutritional products.

Particularly, if you are already using a prescribed medicine, you must work with your physician before you stop using any drug.[29] And don't mix herbal extracts with other drugs. If you wish to consider more natural methods, be certain to discuss it with your health-care provider. Should the physician need more information, discussions of the integrative modalities of treatment mentioned throughout this text cite studies, and suggested readings on related studies are listed, some of which were published in medical journals and in other health-care publications. (See also Appendix A for further resources.)

The Effects of Faith and Prayer

The late David Larson was a medical-religious-spiritual health care researcher, psychiatrist, and president of the National Institute for Healthcare Research. He observed,[30] concerning research into the factors of faith and prayer: "Of three hundred studies on spirituality in scientific journals, the National Institute for Healthcare Research found nearly three-fourths showed that religion had a positive effect on health. Research also shows four out of five patients want doctors to ask them about their faith, and one in two want their doctors to pray with them." Reynolds also reported that of those patients who *USA Today* had surveyed, only 10 percent indicated that their doctors had "talked to them about their faith as a factor in their healing."

A short time later, Carey and Visgaitis,[31] also in *USA Today,* reported on the large numbers of physicians who say that they pray for themselves regularly.

Again, my experience with healing class and workshop students (more with religious or, increasingly, self-described spiritual students than with secular students) supports Larson's position; my observations go slightly beyond his conclusions regarding the desire to discuss their faith and their desire for prayer. More than 80 percent of the people I asked indicated that it was "important" to "very important" that their health-care professionals have an understanding of the impact of the spiritual realm on their health, and a similar percentage wanted their health-care professionals to pray with them.

In a later interview, David Larson[32] said, "most doctors ignore the fact that their patients are fans of God and . . . that 60 percent of the population would like to discuss spiritual issues with their doctors and 40 percent would like their doctors to pray with them."

As is evidenced in Larson's statements above, at least 40 to 50 percent of the general population would like for health professionals to pray with them. So that health professionals know on an individual basis, I suggest that they ask, either on the intake questionnaire or during the first consultation, whether the patient/client would want the practitioner to pray with them.

I am not suggesting that a physician or other health professional proselytize or in any way apply pressure regarding religious views or views of spirituality. However, I am suggesting it may be appropriate to acknowledge the "whole" of a person— body, mind, and spirit—and to allow for the affirming effects of restoring hope, coping, and peacefulness the patient experiences through prayer. The health professional might ask if the patient would like a few minutes of contemplation, meditation, or silence either to begin or to close the consultation. At least, perhaps, the physician might write on the prescription, or *as* a prescription, "Pray 3X per day." (If a patient is an atheist, give them a Dial-A-Prayer number for atheists: no one will answer.)

The Association of Unity Churches International conducted a random survey[33] seeking information similar to that called for by Eisenberg. Raised eyebrows in the medical community and the non-medical community resulted.

With a 40 percent response to the survey of both clerical and lay people, 87 percent reported that they actively participate in their own treatment when they are working with a health-care professional. It may be significant that the same 87 percent prefer the self-descriptor "spiritual" as opposed to the term "religious." Further, 81 percent seek integrative therapies either instead of or concurrent with traditional health care.

The same 87 percent reported above indicate that two major roles they play in their own health care, whether spiritual, physical, or mental, are:

- Deciding *what* category of health-care professional they choose

- Deciding *whom* they choose to work with as a health-care professional

After the facts are gathered, 80 percent pray for guidance about both of these decisions. They hold sacred their individual right to such selection.

As far back as 1965,[34] allopathic physician and psychiatrist John Dorsey's fingernails "ached" with support for personal choice of health-care professionals. He said,

> I cannot imagine what it would be like to be unable to choose my own physician, but I cherish that freedom of choice quite as I cherish my civic right to choose the religious living which I prefer. I consider "taking a physician" to be almost as private and personal a matter as is "taking a mate." Where my health is concerned I need as much harmony of spirit, consent of will, and unification of self-consciousness as I can mobilize, in order to recover and maintain my clear sense of the wholeness/ allness/unity of my human being. Thus, I might not choose you, on account of your extreme subjectivist theories, but if anyone else wished to choose you, I hold that he should not be denied that possibility.

Much of the spiritual population noted above, having made the choice of health-care professionals, tend to carry on brisk conversations with their providers of choice in decision making regarding the type of treatment in which they will participate. More than 80 percent discuss early in the relationship with the chiropractor, nutritionist, osteopath, allopath, homeopath, acupuncturist, or other practitioner how they see their health care being dealt with. They have a deep interest in moving beyond disease management or disease prevention, or even to health maintenance. These people proactively promote their health by incorporating the principles of integrative modalities of treatment.

Those health-care providers who are currently practicing or are cooperating with integrative modalities of health care early in this millennium perhaps are leading the new revolution in science and religion (or spirituality). It truly will be good if they don't now lull themselves into believing that *they* have *the way* toward health and healing.

Resource List of Integrative Modalities of Treatment and Product Sources

MODALITIES

Acupressure

Acupressure Institute
1533 Shattuck Ave.
Berkeley, CA 94709
510-845-1059

Acupuncture/Oriental Medicine

American Association of Oriental Medicine
433 Front St.
Catasauqua, PA 18032
610-266-1433

American Foundation of
Traditional Chinese Medicine
505 Beach St.
San Francisco, CA 94133
415-392-7002

Anthroposophical Medicine

Physician's Association for
Anthroposophical Medicine
5909 SE Division
Portland, OR 97206
503-234-1531

Ayurvedic/Indian Medicine

The Ayurvedic Institute
PO Box 23445
Albuquerque, NM 87192
505-291-9698

Biofeedback

Biofeedback Certification Institute of America
10200 West 44th Ave., Suite 310
Wheat Ridge, CO 80033
303-420-2902

Chelation Therapy

American College for
Advancement in Medicine
23121 Verdugo Dr., Suite 204
Laguna Hills, CA 92653
800-532-3688
www.acam.org

Chiropractic

American Chiropractic Association
1701 Clarendon Blvd.
Arlington, VA 22209
800-986-4636

International Chiropractors Association
1110 North Glebe Rd., Suite 1000
Arlington, VA 22201
703-528-5000

Environmental Medicine

American Academy of Environmental Medicine
7701 E. Kellogg, Suite 625
Wichita, KS 67207
316-684-5500

Feldenkrais Method

The Feldenkrais Guild
3611 SW Hood
Portland, OR 97201
800-775-2118

Hellerwork International
406 Berry St.
Mt. Shasta, CA 96067
800-392-3900

Healing Touch

Healing Touch International, Inc.
445 Union Blvd., Suite 105
Lakewood, CO 80228
www.healingtouch.net

Herbal Medicine

American Botanical Council
PO Box 144345
Austin, TX 78714-4345
512-926-4900

Herb Research Foundation
1007 Pearl St., Suite 200
Boulder, CO 80302
303-449-2265

Holistic Medicine

American Holistic Medical Association
4101 Lake Boone Trail, Suite 201
Raleigh, NC 27607
919-787-5181

American Association of
Naturopathic Physicians
2366 Eastlake Ave E., Suite 32
Seattle, WA 98102
206-323-7610

American Holistic Nurses' Association
PO Box 2130
Flagstaff, AZ 86003
800-278-2462

American Osteopathic Association
142 East Ontario St.
Chicago, IL 60611
312-202-8000

American Polarity Therapy Association
PO Box 19850
Boulder, CO 80308
303-545-2080

Association for Humanistic Psychology
45 Franklin Street, #315
San Francisco, CA 94102
415-864-8850

Homeopathy

National Center for Homeopathy
801 North Fairfax St., Suite 306
Alexandria, VA 22314
703-548-7790

Hypnosis

National Guild of Hypnosis
PO Box 308
Merrimack, NH 03054
603-429-9438

Massage and Bodywork

American Massage Therapy Association
820 Davis Street, Suite 100
Evanston, IL 60201
847-864-0123

International Institute of Reflexology
PO Box 12642
St. Petersburg, FL 33733
727-343-4811

Rolf Institute
205 Canyon Blvd.
Boulder, CO 80302
303-449-5903

Naturopathy

American Association of
Naturopathic Physicians
2366 Eastlake Ave. East, Suite 322
Seattle, WA 98102
317-879-1881

Osteopathic Manipulative Therapy

American Academy of Osteopathy
3500 DePauw Blvd., Suite 1080
Indianapolis, IN 80306
317-879-1881

Reiki

The Reiki Alliance
PO Box 41
Cataldo, ID 83810
208-783-3535

Miscellaneous

The Trager Institute
21 Locust Ave.
Mill Valley, CA 94941
415-388-2688

American Holistic Veterinary Medical Association
2214 Old Emmorton Rd.
Bel Air, MD 21015
410-569-0795

PRODUCTS

Annual Health & Healing Resource Directory

To purchase, write:
Dr. Whitaker's U.S. & Canada Directory
Phillips Publishing, Inc.
7811 Montrose Road
Potomac, MD 20854
800-705-5559

Organic Produce

Eden Acres, Inc.
12100 Lima Center Road
Clinton, MI 49236
517-456-4288
(distributes directories of organic growers)

Radiation Shields for Computer Displays

NoRad Corporation
1549 11th Street
Santa Monica, CA 90401

Alzheimer's Book

Reversing Alzheimer's Naturally
Picoulin Publishing
701 High Street, Suite 206
Auburn, CA 95603

Healing by Hand (Video), God Helps Those Who Help Themselves (Book)

Healers Who Share
9068C Marshal Court
Westminster, CO 80030

A Few of Those Mysterious Initials and to Whom or What They Refer

ABMP—Associated Bodywork & Massage Professionals. Members meet educational and state (if applicable) requirements and agree to adhere to a code of professional ethics. Home office is in Evergreen, Colorado.

AMTA—American Massage Therapy Association. Members have been graduated from an AMTA-accredited or -approved school; received licensing from a state, city, or province; and/or passed the national certification examination administered by the National Certification Board for Therapeutic Massage and Bodywork. Home office is in Evanston, Illinois.

AOBTA—American Oriental Bodywork Therapy Association. Professional-level members have completed not less than five hundred hours of training in oriental bodywork therapy. It represents certified practitioners of several oriental bodywork therapies, including acupuncture. Home offices are based in Voorhees, New Jersey.

ARNP—Advanced Registered Nurse Practitioner.

BSN—Bachelor of Science in Nursing.

CA—Certified Acupuncturist (state certification).

CHt—Certified Hypnotherapist. Certifying organizations include the International Medical and Dental Hypnotherapy Association in Royal Oak, Michigan, and the National Guild of Hypnotists in Merrimack, New Hampshire. Requirements vary.

CISW—Certified Independent Social Worker (a state certification).

CMP/CMT—Certified Massage Practitioner/Certified Massage Therapist. Practitioners receive a certificate of completion from a school of massage therapy.

CNM—Certified Nurse-Midwife. Requires completing an accredited graduate-level nurse-midwifery education program and passing an exam given by the Association of Certified Nurse-Midwife Certification Council. Prior to taking the national certification exam, the candidate must be a licensed registered nurse (RN).

CR(1)—Certified Reflexologist. Must have passed an examination given by the International Institute of Reflexology (IIR) in St. Petersburg, Florida. To qualify for the examination, one must take three IIR two-day seminars and have one year of practice from the first seminar. To maintain certification, CRs must attend one IIR seminar at least every third year.

CR(2)—Certified Rolfer. Requires fifteen weeks of training at the Rolf Institute. Prerequisite for the training, one must have college-level understanding of anatomy, physiology, and kinesiology.

DC—Doctor of Chiropractic. Degree requires at least four years of training at an accredited chiropractic college. Chiropractors take both state and national board examinations and are licensed to practice by state.

DHANP—Diplomate of the Homeopathic Academy of Naturopathic Physicians. Naturopathic doctors who pass the certification examination given by the Homeopathic Academy of Naturopathic Physicians may use these initials to indicate that they are also homeopaths.

DO—Doctor of Osteopathy. One must complete four years of training at a college of osteopathic medicine. There are currently sixteen such colleges throughout the United States accredited by the American Osteopathic Association in Chicago, Illinois.

DOM—Doctor of Oriental Medicine.

DVM—Doctor of Veterinary Medicine.

GCFP—Guild Certified Feldenkrais Practitioner. Requires completion of a professional training program accredited by The Feldenkrais Guild, active practice of the Feldenkrais method, and continuing educational experience. Granted by The Feldenkrais Guild in Albany, Oregon.

LAc, LicAc—Licensed Acupuncturist. Normally indicates state licensure; may also indicate a diploma from a European school.

LCSW—Licensed Clinical Social Worker or Licensed Certified Social Worker (state license).

LMFT—Licensed Marriage and Family Therapist. A mental health professional who treats mental illness and life issues from a family systems perspective. Treatment takes into account family relationships and dynamics, whether working with an individual, a couple, or a family.

LMP/LMT—Licensed Massage Practitioner/Licensed Massage Therapist (state license). Some states license bodyworkers as massage practitioners, while other states license them as massage therapists.

LPN—Licensed Practical Nurse. They complete post-high-school education of about a year that focuses on basic nursing care; also must pass a licensing examination. LPNs are not registered nurses.

MAc—Master of Acupuncture. There are seven such educational programs accredited by the National Accreditation Commission for

Schools and Colleges of Acupuncture and Oriental Medicine, based in Silver Spring, Maryland.

MOM—Master of Oriental Medicine. Graduate of an MOM education program. There are nineteen such programs accredited by the National Accreditation Commission for Schools and Colleges of Acupuncture and Oriental Medicine.

MPH—Master of Public Health.

MSH—Master of Science in Nursing.

MSW—Master of Social Work.

NAET—Nambudripads Allergy Elimination Techniques. For information regarding allergies as a cause of numerous ailments and how to eliminate them, see NAET in Appendix C.

ND—Doctor of Naturopathy. NDs are currently licensed in eleven states—Alaska, Arizona, Connecticut, Hawaii, Maine, Montana, New Hampshire, Oregon, Utah, Vermont, and Washington. These states require NDs to graduate from a school accredited by the Council on Naturopathic Medical Education or an equivalent foreign school.

NP/ARNP—Nurse Practitioner/Advanced Registered Nurse Practitioner. A registered nurse (RN) who has completed a nurse practitioner education program, most often a master's degree program in addition to the two to four years of basic nursing education required of all RNs.

OD—Doctor of Optometry.

OMD/DOM—Oriental Medical Doctor/Doctor of Oriental Medicine. Normally, these titles indicate additional training beyond state licensure to practice acupuncture. These titles are sometimes taken by Chinese MDs who are licensed in China but not in the United States, and by U.S. practitioners who complete OMD or DOM degree programs at foreign schools.

PA—Physician Assistant. One graduates from an accredited physician assistant or surgeon assistant educational program (often two years in length). Most states also require that PAs be nationally certified by the National Commission on Certification of Physician Assistants.

PT—Physical Therapist. Prerequisite to this state license, one must complete an educational program accredited by the Commission on Accreditation in Physical Therapy Education.

RD—Registered Dietitian. One must have a minimum of four years' education and training in dietetics or a related field at a university accredited by the American Dietetic Association in Chicago, Illinois; they also must pass an examination given by the Commission on Dietetic Registration, and maintain continuing educational requirements to maintain the title.

RM—Reiki Master. The general criteria to be a Reiki Master include at least three years as a Reiki practitioner and at least one year as an apprentice to a Reiki Master. Many RMs belong to The Reiki Alliance in Cataldo, Idaho, whose members uphold professional standards. The organization does not offer certification.

RN—Registered Nurse. Requires graduating from a state-approved school of nursing (two to four years in length) and passing a state licensing examination.

Resources on the Web—A Sampling of the Most Trustworthy

Ask Dr. Weil: The website of Andrew Weil, M.D. includes the "Ask Dr. Weil" daily Q &A column and others of his writings as well as links to other resources. The site features a directory of herbalists and other practitioners of alternative medicine. *www.drweil.com*

FeMiNa Health and Wellness is a major resource for women's issues. The "Ask a Woman Doctor" link connects you to women physicians, and other links provide contact information for women's health clinics, midwives, massage therapists, and other women's health-care providers throughout the United States and Canada. *www.pbs.org/bodyandsoul/events.htm*

HealthGate: This source contains material on both alternative and conventional medicine. The "Patient Education" page connects you to guides to medical tests, surgeries, and prescription and over-the-counter drugs. *www.healthgate.com*

HealthWorld Online: Combines allopathic and alternative medicine: information on wellness, self-care, fitness, nutrition, and exercise. Professional referral network is also provided. *www.healthy.net*

Homeopathy Home Page: Attempts to provide links to every homeopathy resource available; it probably comes close. *www.homeopathy home.com*

Traditional Indian Medicine: Focuses on Chinese herbal medicine but also provides information on the Ayurvedic, Tibetan, Native American, and Thai traditions. *www.mic.ki.se/china.html*

The International Center for Reiki Training: Designed primarily for Reiki students and practitioners, but includes history, principles, and uses for this form of energy healing. *www.reiki.org*

Mayo Health Oasis: Spans a wide range of topics. www.MayoClinic.com

NAET: Nambudripads Allergy Elimination Techniques. *www.naet.com*

NCCAM: National Institutes of Health's National Center for Complementary and Alternative Medicine includes information on research grants and their clearinghouse, which disseminates information on complementary and alternative medicine to practitioners as well as to the public. *nccam.nih.gov*

OncoLink: University of Pennsylvania's Cancer Center features information on cancer causes, screening and prevention, clinical trials of new treatments, and financial issues for patients and their families, as well as coping with grief and loss. *oncolink.org*

Yahoo!'s Alternative Medicine page offers links to numerous indices, organizations, and practitioners of various alternative health modalities, as well as short reviews of the best sites. *www.yahoo.com/health/ alternative_medicine*

Notes

1. Eisenberg, D. *Encounters with Qi: Exploring Chinese Medicine.* New York: Norton and Company. 1995.

2. Taber, C.W. *Cyclopedic Medical Dictionary.* Philadelphia: F. A. Davis Company. 1960. p. A-39.

3. Larson, D. Oral report to Humility in Theology Information Center. 1998.

4. Weil, A. *Journal of Integrative Medicine*, highlighted in newsletter "Self Healing." March 1999.

5. Holland, A. V*oices of Qi: An Introductory Guide to Traditional Chinese Medicine.* Seattle: Northwest Institute of Acupuncture & Oriental Medicine. 1997. p. 62.

6. Cohen, K. *The Way of Qigong: The Art and Science of Chinese Energy Healing.* New York: Ballantine Books. 1997.

7. Dossey, L. Personal conversation. 1997.

8. Dossey, L. *Reinventing Medicine: Beyond Mind-Body to a New Era of Healing.* Harper San Francisco: Harper Collins Publishers. 1999. pp. 16–26.

9. Mosley, G., and Hill, J. *The Power of Prayer around the World.* Philadelphia and London: Templeton Foundation Press. 2000.

10. Benson, H. *Timeless Healing: The Power and Biology of Belief.* New York: Scribner. 1996. p. 127.

11. Borysenko, J. Minding the Body, Mending the Mind. Recording of lecture at Chautauqua, New York. 1996.

12. Templeton, J. *Agape Love: A Tradition Found in Eight World Religions.* Philadelphia and London: Templeton Foundation Press. 1999.

13. Worthington, E., Jr., et al., eds. *Dimensions of Forgiveness: Psychological Research & Theological Perspectives.* Philadelphia and London: Templeton Foundation Press. 1998.

14. Fox, E. *The Sermon on the Mount.* New York: Harper & Brothers Publishing. 1938.

15. Eisenberg, D. *Encounters with Qi: Exploring Chinese Medicine.* New York: Norton and Company. 1995. pp. 240–241.

16. Simonton, C., Matthews-Simonton, S., and Creighton, J. Why some people recover and others die when the diagnosis is the same for each. *New Woman.* Sept.–Oct. 1978. p. 34.

17. Poznanski-Hutchison, C. Healing Touch International's official response to the April 1, 1998, *JAMA* article "debunking" therapeutic touch. *Colorado Center for Healing Touch Inc. Newsletter.* May 1998: 8: 1, 3, 4.

18. Rosa, L, Rosa, E., Sarner, L., and Barrett, S. A close look at therapeutic touch. *Journal of the American Medical Association.* April 1998: 279: 13.

19. Mosley, G., and Hill, J. *The Power of Prayer around the World.* Philadelphia and London: Templeton Foundation Press. 2000.

20. Shamsuddin, A.M. *IP6: Nature's Revolutionary Cancer-Fighter.* New York: Kensington Books. 1998.

21. Templeton, J. *Possibilities for Over One Hundredfold More Spiritual Information: The Humble Approach in Theology and Science.* Philadelphia and London: Templeton Foundation Press. 2000.

22. Weil, A. *Spontaneous Healing.* New York: Fawcett Columbine. 1995. pp. 23–24

23. Campbell, C. Thornton, K; Fortney, W., Consultant. *The Country Vet's Home Remedies for Dogs.* Lincolnwood, Illinois: Publications International, Ltd. 1998.

24. D'Adamo, P.J. *Eat Right 4 Your Type: The Individualized Diet to Staying Healthy, Living Longer, and Achieving Your Ideal Weight.* New York: G.P. Putnam's Sons. 1996.

25. Cranton, E.M. Chelation Therapy: New Hope for Victims of Arteriosclerosis and Age-Associated Diseases. Pamphlet. Laguna Hills, California: American College for Advancement in Medicine. n.d. p. 2.

26. Koenig, H.G., Bearon, L., and Dayringer, R. Physician perspectives on the role of religion in the physician–older patient relationship. *Journal of Family Practice.* 1989: 28: 441–448.

27. Picoulin, K. *Reversing Alzheimer's Naturally.* Auburn, California: Picoulin Publications. 1996.

28. Kroeger, H. *God Helps Those Who Help Themselves.* Denver: Hanna Kroeger Publications. 1997.

29. Murray, M. *Natural Alternatives to Prozac.* New York: William Morrow and Company. 1996.

30. Reynolds, B. Prayer: The medicine patients are seeking. Interview with D. Larson. *USA Today.* 1996: May 3: 10A.

31. Carey, A., and Visgaitis, G. Doctors pray for selves. *USA Today.* 1997: March 27: 2A.

32. Cohen, J. The greatest story never told. Interview with David Larson. *Utne Reader.* 1997: March–April: 70.

33. Association of Unity Churches. Random survey of 1,960 Unity ministers, licensed teachers, and congregants; 781 responses. Lee's Summit, Missouri. 1997.

34. Dorsey, J.M. *Illness or Allness: Conversations of a Psychiatrist.* Detroit: Wayne State University Press. 1965. pp. 445–446.

Suggested Readings and Other References

Althoff, S., Williams, P., Molvig, D., and Schuster, L. *A Guide to Alternative Medicine*. Lincolnwood, Illinois: Publications International. 1997.

American Demographics. *Toplines: Quackery No More: Alternative Medicine Moves into the Mainstream*. Gardyn, R., ed. January 2001. pp. 10–11.

Batmanghelidj, F. *Your Body's Many Cries for Water: You Are Not Sick, You Are Thirsty*. 2nd ed. Falls Church, Virginia: Global Health Solutions, Inc. 1997.

Bearon, L.B., and Koenig, H.G. Religious cognitions and use of prayer in health and illness. *The Gerontologist*. 1990: 30(2): 249–253.

Borysenko, J., and Borysenko, M. *The Power of the Mind to Heal*. Carlsbad, CA: Hay House, Inc., Publishers. 1994.

Brennan, B. *Hands of Light: A Guide to Healing through the Human Energy Field*. New York: Bantam Books. 1988.

Byrd, R.C. Positive therapeutic effects of intercessory prayer in a coronary care unit population. *Southern Medical Journal.* 1988: 81(7): 826–830.

Carrel, A. *The Voyage to Lourdes.* New York: Harper & Bros. 1941.

Carter, M., and Weber, T. *One Touch Healing.* Revised. Paramus, New Jersey: Reward Books. 2000.

D'Adamo, P.J. *Cook Right 4 Your Type: The Practical Kitchen Companion to Eat Right 4 Your Type.* New York: G.P. Putnam's Sons. 1998.

D'Adamo, P.J. *Eat Right 4 Your Baby: The Individualized Guide to Fertility and Maximum Health During Pregnancy, Nursing, and Your Baby's First Year.* New York: G.P. Putnam's Sons. 2003.

D'Adamo, P.J. *Eat Right 4 Your Type: The Individualized Diet to Staying Healthy, Living Longer, and Achieving Your Ideal Weight.* New York: G.P. Putnam's Sons. 1996.

D'Adamo, P.J. *Eat Right 4 Your Type Complete Blood Type Encyclopedia.* New York: Riverhead Books. 2002.

D'Adamo, P.J. *Live Right 4 Your Type: The Individualized Prescription for Maximizing Health, Metabolism, and Vitality in Every Stage of Your Life.* New York: G.P. Putnam's Sons. 2001.

Dossey, L. *Healing Words.* New York: Harper Collins. 1993.

Dossey, L. *Prayer Is Good Medicine.* Harper San Francisco Publishers. 1996.

Dossey, L. Who gets sick and who gets well. *Alternative Therapies in Health and Medicine.* 1995: Vol. 1, pp. 6–11.

Fillmore, C. *Christian Healing.* Unity Village, Missouri: Unity House. 1979.

Fillmore, M. *Myrtle Fillmore's Healing Letters*. Unity Village, Missouri: Unity House. 1981.

Gartner, J., Larson, D.B., and Vachar-Mayberry, C.D. A systematic review of the quantity and quality of empirical research published in four pastoral counseling journals: 1975–84. *The Journal of Pastoral Care*. 1990: 44(2): 115–123.

Harpur, T. *The Uncommon Touch: An Investigation of Spiritual Healing*. Cleveland, OH: McClelland & Stewart, Inc. 1994.

Energy Research Group, comps., *High Frequency Model for Kirlian Photography*. New York: Energy Research Group. 1973.

Holzer, H. *The Secret of Healing*. Hillsboro, Oregon: Beyond Words Publishing, Inc. 1995.

Hover, K.D., Mentgen, J., and Scandrett-Hibdon, S. *Healing Touch: A Resource for Health Care Professionals*. Denver: Delmar Publishers. 1995.

Jafolla, R., and Jafolla, M.A. *Nourishing the Life Force*. Unity Village, Missouri: Unity House. 1983.

Koenig, H.G., *Aging and God: Spiritual Pathways to Mental Health in Midlife and Later Years*. New York – London – Norwood (Australia): The Haworth Pastoral Press. 1994.

Koenig, H.G., ed. *Handbook of Religion and Mental Health*. San Diego: Academic Press. 1998.

Koenig, H.G. Research on religion and mental health in later life: A review and commentary. *Journal of Geriatric Psychiatry*. 1990: 23(1): 23–53.

King, D.G. Religion and health relationships: A review. *Journal of Religion and Health*. 1990: 29(20): 101–112.

Krieger, D. *Accepting Your Power to Heal.* Santa Fe, New Mexico: Bear & Company Publishers. 1993.

Krieger, D. *The Therapeutic Touch.* Englewood Cliffs, New Jersey: Prentice-Hall. 1979.

Kroeger, H. *New Dimensions in Healing Yourself.* Denver: Hanna Kroeger Publications. 1996.

Kroeger, H. *The Basic Causes of Modern Diseases and How to Remedy Them.* Carlsbad, California: Hay House, Inc. 1998.

Larson, D., Sherrill, K., and Lyon, J. Neglect and misuse of the 'R word': Systematic reviews of religious measures in health, mental health and aging research. In: Levin, J.S., ed. *Religion in Aging and Health: Theoretical Foundations and Methodological Frontiers.* Newbury Park, California: Sage Publications. 1993.

Levin, J.S., and Vanderpool, H.Y. Religious factors in physical health and the prevention of illness. *Prevention in Human Services.* 1991: 9(2): 41–63.

MacNutt, F. *Healing.* Knoxville, TN: Ave Maria Press. 1991.

Matthews, D.A., Larson, D.B., and Barry, C.P. The faith factor: An annotated bibliography of clinical research on spiritual subjects. Rockville, Maryland: National Institute for Healthcare Research. 1993.

Mosley, G.R. *A Comparison of Secular and Religious Experiential Education Activities in the Adult Religious Education Classroom.* Columbus, Ohio: ERIC, Ohio State University. 1980.

Mosley, G.R. Benefits of religion: Unity. In: Kutscher, A.H., ed. *Religion and Bereavement: Counsel, Thoughts for the Clergyman.* New York: Health Sciences Publishing Corp. 1972.

Mosley, G.R. *Living with Loss* (pamphlet). Lee's Summit, Missouri: Unity House. 2000.

Mosley, G.R. Religion and mental health from the Unity perspective. In: Koenig, H.G., ed. *Handbook of Religion and Mental Health*. San Diego: Academic Press. 1998.

Mosley, G.R *Unity Methods of Self-Exploration*. Detroit: Ducat Publishing. 1975.

Motoyama, Dr. H. *The Functional Relationship between Yoga Asanas and Acupuncture Meridians*. Tokyo, Japan: I.A.R.P. 1979.

Motz, J. *Hands of Life: An Energy Healer Reveals the Secrets of Using Your Body's Own Energy Medicine for Healing, Recovery, and Transformation*. New York: Bantam Books. 1998.

Nelda, S., Ed.D., R.N. The experience of receiving therapeutic touch. *Journal of Advanced Nursing*. 1992: 17651–17667.

PapOn, R.D. *Homeopathy Made Simple*. Charlottesville, Virginia: Hampton Roads Publishing Co. 1998.

Poloma, M.M., and Pendleton, B.F. The effects of prayer and prayer experiences on measures of general well-being. *Journal of Psychology and Theology*. 1991: 19(1): 71–83.

Ravitz, L.J. Application of the electrodynamic field theory in biology, psychiatry, medicine and hypnosis: I. General survey. *American Journal of Clinical Hypnosis*. 1959: 1: 135–150.

Rubick, B. Can Western science provide a foundation for acupuncture? (Keynote address from the 1993 Symposium of the American Academy of Medical Acupuncture (AAMA). *AAMA Review*. Spring/Summer, 1993: 5(1): 26–27.

Sanford, A. *The Healing Light*. New York: First Ballantine Books. 1991.

Simonton, C.O., Matthews-Simonton, S., and Creighton, J. Why some people recover and others die when the diagnosis is the same for each. *New Woman*. Sept.–Oct., 1978, pp. 24-36.

Slater, D. *Healing by Hand.* Video, Vols. I and II. Denver: Healers Who Share. n.d.

Solisti-Mattelon, K., and Mattelon, P. *The Holistic Animal Handbook.* Hillsboro, Oregon: Words Publishing, Inc. 2000.

Templeton, J.M., Sr., and Herrmann, R.L. *The God Who Would Be Known: Revelation of the Divine in Contemporary Science.* San Francisco: Harper & Row. 1989.

Thomas, Z. *Healing Touch: The Church's Forgotten Language.* Phoenix, AZ, Westminster John Knox Press. 1994.

Tiwari, M. *Ayurveda: A Life of Balance.* Rochester, Vermont: Healing Arts Press. 1995.

Weil, A. *Ask Dr. Weil.* New York: The Ballantine Publishing Group. 1998.

Williamson, G., and Williamson, D. *Transformative Rituals: Celebrations for Personal Growth.* Deerfield Beach, Florida: Health Communications, Inc. 1994.

Native American

Garrett, J.T., and Garrett, M.T. *Medicine of the Cherokee: The Way of Right Relationship.* Santa Fe, New Mexico: Bear & Company. 1996.

Kavasch, E.G., and Baar, K. *American Indian Healing Arts: Herbs Rituals, and Remedies for Every Season of Life.* New York: Bantam Books. 1999.

Rain, Mary Summer. *Spirit Song: The Introduction of No-Eyes.* Norfolk, Virginia: Hampton Roads Publishing Co., Inc. 1993.

An Open Invitation to You, the Reader

Whether you are a professional health-care provider with years of experience and service or you have just begun a search for integrative modalities of treatment for yourself or friends and family, I would like to hear of ways you use or have used Healing Hover Touch. Please also share the outcomes with me.

In telling the story of what you did and the results achieved, please indicate whether or not I have your permission to use the story either in print or orally. To avoid my possibly assigning a fictitious name that really wasn't fictitious, please give me the real names of people. If the story is used, unless you tell me in writing otherwise, I will change the names and, when appropriate to maintain confidentiality, also the gender. If the story is used in print, I will endeavor to inform each contributor where it has been or will be used.

If I may use your actual name, please state that in your email. If others are involved who are willing to have their actual names used, please provide me with a statement to that effect along with both site and email addresses, and a telephone number(s).

Please also provide a brief description of your involvement in healing practices—e.g., chiropractor, physician, nurse, reflexologist, veterinarian, beginner or experienced in healing or nutritional therapy, layperson, Reiki Master, dietitian, or other practitioner.

Please email to:

Glenn R. Mosley: glenn.mosley@charter.net

Digital Video Disks (100 minutes in length) demonstrating the principles of the material in this volume are available for purchase. When you write, place your order if interested in them. $12 each; ask about discounts for volume purchase of five or more.

About the Author

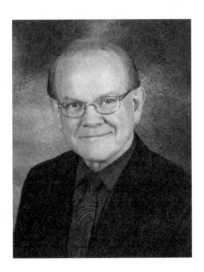

The Reverend Dr. Glenn R. Mosley first studied biology and microbiology as an intended precursor to a career in medicine before he became involved in psychosocial studies. He is a graduate of the State University of New York (Excelsior College, Albany) and holds two degrees from Wayne State University in Michigan. His Ph.D. in education, with emphasis on trans-cultural, trans-racial, and interpersonal communications, is from Walden University. He also has a Doctor of Ministry degree. He holds an M.Sc. from Central Michigan University and has done postdoctoral studies at the University of Michigan, Harvard, M.I.T., Princeton, Stanford, and Penn State. He holds an honorary doctorate as well. Dr. Mosley is a graduate of, and has been ordained by, the Unity School of Christianity, and he is president emeritus of the Association of Unity Churches International. He has traveled in all fifty states and in nearly sixty countries, lecturing to religious, medical (including the American Academy of Family Physicians), and secular groups in most of them.

Mosley has taught death, dying, and coping strategies (thanatology); he also taught integrative healing modalities as an adjunct professor to Akron University's teaching consortium of schools, hospitals, and nursing facilities in northeast Ohio. In New York, he was a founding board member with Dr. Elisabeth Kubler-Ross and Dr. Austin Kutscher and served on the editorial board of The Foundation of Thanatology. He has authored or coauthored twelve books, and he has contributed to six others; he has written three hundred-plus monographs and articles. He is a Templeton Foundation Board member and a former judge for the Templeton Prize for Progress in Religion.

Dr. Mosley is a member of the American Association for the Advancement of Science and the Union of Concerned Scientists for Environmental Solutions. He is listed in *The International Who's Who in Theology and Science,* 1992 and 1996 editions; *Who's Who in Religion*, 1992–1993 edition; *Who's Who in America*, 1992–1993, 1999, and 2000; and *International Who's Who of Professionals*, 1996.

Sentient Publications, LLC publishes books on cultural creativity, experimental education, transformative spirituality, holistic health, new science, and ecology, approached from an integral viewpoint. Our authors are intensely interested in exploring the nature of life from fresh perspectives, addressing life's great questions, and fostering the full expression of the human potential. Sentient Publications' books arise from the spirit of inquiry and the richness of the inherent dialogue between writer and reader.

We are very interested in hearing from our readers. To direct suggestions or comments to us, or to be added to our mailing list, please contact:

SENTIENT PUBLICATIONS, LLC
1113 Spruce Street
Boulder, CO 80302
303.443.2188
contact@sentientpublications.com
www.sentientpublications.com